Aging Naturally

how to slow down
the aging process
and boost your
vitality

Aging

Naturally

jennifer amerena

photography by liz m^caulay and michelle garrett

This edition published by Hermes House,
an imprint of Anness Publishing Limited
Hermes House, 88–89 Blackfriars Road,
London SE1 8HA

© Anness Publishing Limited 2001
Updated © 2002

Published in the USA by Hermes House,
Anness Publishing Inc.
27 West 20th Street,
New York, NY 10011

A CIP catalogue record for this book is available
from the British Library.

Publisher: Joanna Lorenz
Project Editor: Melanie Halton
Managing Editor: Helen Sudell
Designer: Andrew Nash
Photographers: Liz Mcaulay and Michelle Garrett
Stylist: Suzanne Rose
Picture Credit: gettyone Stone (p. 8cl)

10 9 8 7 6 5 4 3 2 1

Contents

Chapter 1

Understanding aging 6

Chapter 2

The anti-aging diet 14

Chapter 3

Staying fit throughout life 32

Chapter 4

Looking after the body 44

Chapter 5

Taking care of your appearance 70

Chapter 6

The menopause 82

Health checks 94

Index 96

Understanding aging

We can now expect to live longer and better than any generation before us. In every decade of the 20th century the average human life span rose by about two years. This means that middle age is being re-defined and we can now consider ourselves young until our 50s and beyond. The challenge that we face as individuals is to age in the best way possible: to ignore negative stereotypes associated with age, to understand why our bodies change and to actively take charge of our health.

Older and wiser

In many cultures advancing age is viewed as a time of wisdom. Older people are seen as adept at solving problems or, if they cannot solve them, at developing coping strategies. They are considered skilled at adapting to situations, knowing when to rest and when to pursue goals (and knowing which goals are worth pursuing), controlling anger and supporting and nurturing others. They are respected for the experience and knowledge that they can impart to younger generations. But these attitudes are not true of all cultures. In the West, for example, there is a tendency to see older people negatively: as less useful, efficient, capable and attractive than their younger counterparts.

△ Many cultures appreciate the wisdom, social interaction and playfulness offered by older members of the extended family.

attitudes towards women

Society differs in its attitudes towards aging in men and in women. Whereas men may be accorded status and respect as they grow older women may feel as though they gradually become invisible. Older women are often poorly represented in the media

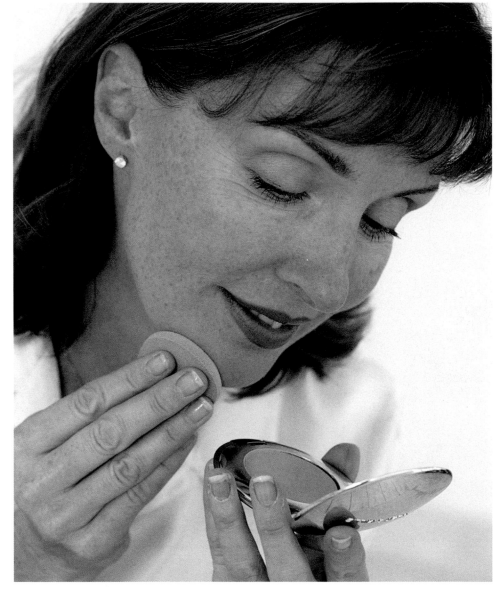

△ Make-up can help you to feel good about yourself, but is more flattering if kept light and natural looking.

and there is a shortage of older female role models. There is a strong tendency in the West to attribute value and status to youth and beauty. Aging, especially in women, is often seen as a loss of vitality and sexual attractiveness. Women may feel encouraged to fight the body changes that accompany aging with restricted diets, cosmetic products and even surgery.

valuing ourselves

Despite negative attitudes from society, it is our collective responsibility to value ourselves as individuals and provide our

children and grandchildren with positive models of aging. Our 40s and 50s are a time of life when we have plenty of experience behind us and half a lifetime still ahead of us. Advances in healthcare, housing and working conditions mean that we can look forward to an active and healthy old age.

Growing older often brings new freedom from responsibilities. Children leaving home is a major milestone in middle or later life and one that can often provoke mixed feelings. Try to focus on the positive, however. If you find yourself with new-found freedom, decide carefully how you

◁ Gardening is a gentle form of exercise, which can bring enjoyment and a sense of real achievement.

should spend it. Ask yourself what your future goals should be. Would you like to go on an exotic vacation, take up yoga or join a gym? Would you like to learn a new skill or return to study? Would you like to train for a new career, start a business or learn about new technology? Perhaps you would like to revive an old hobby that you have neglected for many years. The choices are yours and they are endless.

Relationships can take on heightened importance as we grow older and have more time to devote to them. We may re-discover companionship with a partner, forge new relationships with adult

△ Grandparents can enjoy relaxed fun time with children, free from the pressures of parenthood.

children, revive old friendships or become grandparents for the first time. Alternatively, we may find the strength to leave relationships that are unfulfilling.

in the future

People are making increasingly better financial provision for later life with the result that there is a growing population of people with money to spend and plenty of leisure time. Companies are beginning to recognize that the over-40s are a wealthy group to target. As a result, leisure options for older people are increasing.

In recent decades the West has embraced preventative and holistic healthcare. Increasingly, people are educated about the importance of diet and exercise. The knowledge we need to take responsibility for our health is now readily available.

The fight against aging

The quest to extend the human life span is nothing new; scientists have long searched for ways to prevent aging and cure life-threatening illnesses such as cancer. Significant progress is being made in the field of gerontology and it is likely that in the future we will be able to slow the aging process down and live actively into old age. For example, in 1999, Italian researchers at the European Institute of Oncology in Milan published findings regarding the existence of a genetic defect in mice that causes them to live a third longer than other mice. The mice ate a normal diet and had a normal body weight but they lacked a gene for a specific protein. The implications of this finding for human life spans is the focus of intensive research.

taking care for your health

As you grow older it is important to be aware of the changes that take place in your body. You need to know how to prevent problems occurring and how to respond to them when they do. Taking responsibility for your own health and wellbeing gives you a powerful sense of control and self-confidence. However, this does not mean excluding healthcare professionals. For example, tell your doctor if you are taking herbal medicines. Other factors which may help include:

• Listening to your body and responding appropriately.
• Learning about complementary therapies and how they can help you prevent and treat health problems.
• Exercising regularly and concentrating on staying flexible and active rather than "going for the burn".
• Eating plenty of fruit and vegetables.
• Understanding the age-related changes that affect each body system. Learn which changes can be prevented, which ones should be accommodated and which changes may be early warning signs of health problems.

positive avoidance

Many of the harmful aspects of life have been identified, which means that we can now make a positive effort to avoid the things that cause us harm. For example, stress, cigarette smoking, drinking too much alcohol and long-term exposure to the sun and pollution are five of the major contributors to the aging process. Even if we eat healthy food, exercise regularly and have plenty of sleep, these factors will still have an adverse effect on the body.

Fortunately, it is comparatively easy to avoid cigarette smoking, excessive alcohol consumption and exposure to the sun. It is less easy to avoid pollution and stress; these are things that we need to tackle collectively, and this is now recognized and taken seriously by scientists, employers and governments. Also, even if can we cannot avoid stress and pollution there are ways of mitigating their effects on the body. There is a wide range of complementary therapies that can help us to relax and there is some evidence that taking antioxidant supplements can mitigate the damaging effects of environmental pollution.

complementary therapies

In the past, remedies for illness were passed down from one generation to the next in a strong tradition of herbal medicine. Although people may not have known how plant remedies worked, they remained tried and trusted ways of treating illness. For example, St John's wort was used as an antidepressant long before science taught us about serotonin, a brain chemical that affects mood. A report in the *British Medical Journal* stated that St John's wort has fewer side effects than imipramine, a widely prescribed antidepressant.

▽ **Acupressure can be particularly helpful for pain control, treatment of common ailments and boosting the immune system to help protect the body from disease.**

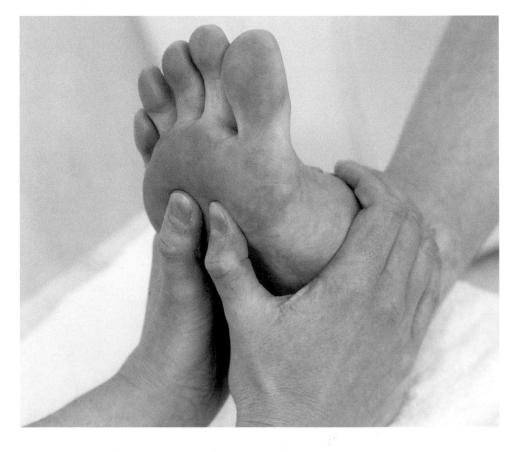

△ **St John's Wort is a natural antidepressant, but prolonged use may cause photosensitivity.**

Although conventional medicine remains the first option for many people during sickness, there is a move towards complementary therapies that treat the body as an interdependent whole rather than a collection of individual parts. It is now thought that many plant remedies are effective because they contain ingredients that work in concert with one another. In contrast, most Western drugs simply isolate the active ingredient in a plant.

Herbalism is just one of many types of complementary therapy available. Other types of recommended treatment include aromatherapy, massage, hypnotherapy, reflexology, dietary medicine and acupuncture. Complementary therapies are now recognized by many doctors and scientists as being valuable aids in assisting the body to fight illness and aging.

▷ **As we age our bodies become less supple and taking the time to undertake gentle stretching exercises each day is a good way of maintaining muscle and joint flexibility.**

The harmful effects of free radicals

◁ **When buying sun tan lotion keep your skin type in mind. Many fair-skinned people begin to suffer skin damage after just 10 minutes in the sun. By buying a factor 10 sunscreen they can multiply this time by 10, and benefit from up to 100 minutes protection, before damage begins to occur.**

Although the causes of aging are not entirely understood, we now know that damage to the body by substances known as free radicals plays a critical role. In fact, doctors and nutritionists say that, without doubt, the most important fight against aging should be against free radical damage. Although free radicals have received much press attention, few of us understand exactly what they are or how they affect the body.

free radicals

Oxygen is essential for life, but it can also be considered a poison. This is because when oxygen is used for essential processes inside the body, it leads to the production of damaging molecules known as free radicals. The most damaging characteristic of free radicals is their chemical structure in that they contain an unpaired electron. This means that they roam around the body "searching" for healthy molecules to pair with. Unfortunately, this pairing process damages the host molecule and irreversibly changes the DNA (material that carries genetic information). If free radicals are allowed to damage body cells in this way over a long period of time, the result is extensive cell damage and aging, as well as diseases such as arthritis, heart disease, cataracts and cancer.

A good way to understand free radical damage to the body is to think of it as continuous internal radiation. Yet free radicals are not just created by normal bodily processes; they are also created by oxidation outside the body. For example, combustion processes, radiation from the sun, cigarette smoking and environmental pollution all give rise to free radicals. Also, some foods and drinks (fried food and alcohol, for example) generate more free radicals than others.

the fight against free radicals

Although our bodies have evolved their own defences against free radicals, it is essential that we minimize exposure to free radicals where possible. This means giving up cigarette smoking (and avoiding other people's cigarette smoke), not eating burnt food, staying out of direct sunlight, not drinking too much alcohol and minimizing exposure to environmental pollution such as traffic fumes. It is also believed that sleep deprivation can increase free radical damage to the body, so we need to make sure we have sufficient sleep every night.

the best weapons: antioxidants

By far the best weapons in the war against free radicals are antioxidants, which are found in vitamins A, C and E, in co-enzyme Q10 and betacarotene, as well as in minerals such as selenium and zinc.

When free radicals are roaming around the body, antioxidant molecules can pair with them, preventing them from attacking healthy molecules. When antioxidants pair with (or "mop up") roaming free radicals they can then be eliminated from the body via the excretory systems. This way, no damage is done to the body.

One way to understand the action of antioxidants is to observe what happens when lemon juice is dropped onto the cut surface of an apple. As soon as the apple is cut and exposed to the air it reacts with oxygen and starts to discolour. Yet if lemon juice is squeezed onto the cut surface, the antioxidant action of the vitamin C in the juice will prevent the discoloration. However, this protection is only temporary and the cut surfaces will start to oxidize as the antioxidant function wears down.

The importance of antioxidants in your diet cannot be over-estimated. It is crucial for everyone, especially older people, to eat foods rich in antioxidant vitamins and minerals. Nutritionists recommend eating plenty of fresh fruit and vegetables on a daily basis. Antioxidants are also available in the form of supplements.

△ Strawberries contain a phytochemical called ellagic acid which is believed to fight against cancer.

▽ The darker outer leaves of lettuce contain betacarotene, an antioxidant thought to protect against some cancers.

Where to find antioxidants

The main antioxidant nutrients are vitamins A, C, and E, zinc and selenium. Foods containing these vitamins and minerals should be part of your daily diet. In addition to these vitamins and minerals, there are other substances known as phytochemicals, found in plants, that also have antioxidant properties. These include bioflavanoids (found in citrus fruit) and lycopene (found in tomatoes). Some amino acids, such as cysteine and glutamic acid also have antioxidant effects. Cysteine and glutamic acid are found in white meat, tuna, lentils, beans, nuts, seeds, onions and garlic.

The following foods are excellent sources of antioxidants and can be eaten in abundance:

- Sweet potatoes
- Carrots
- Watercress
- Broccoli
- Peas
- Cauliflower
- Tomatoes
- Citrus fruit
- Watermelon
- Strawberries
- Seeds
- Nuts

The anti-aging diet

The food we eat can make a huge contribution to our health and wellbeing. The science of nutrition has made huge advances in recent decades. We now know how to help prevent many aging-related problems, such as heart disease, by concentrating on some food groups in the diet and limiting others. It is also possible that taking dietary supplements and restricting daily calorie intake can enhance life as we grow older.

Revising your eating habits

Between the ages of 40 and 65, life becomes more sedentary for many of us. We may retire and have fewer personal obligations than before. A slower lifestyle means that the body needs fewer calories. Yet our vitamin and mineral requirements remain the same or increase in order to prevent cell aging and dietary deficiencies.

healthy eating patterns

Since diet is so important as you get older, it is advisable to periodically alter your diet and eating patterns. Do you eat with health in mind or are your eating habits based on convenience? Are you prone to eating lots of "empty calories" in the form of fatty and sugary foods? Are you at risk of diet-related health problems such as osteoporosis (a chronic disease that weakens the bones)?

Nutritionists recommend a low-fat diet based on fresh fruit and vegetables, unrefined, complex carbohydrates and protein foods such as oily fish. This keeps the immune system in good working order and helps to prevent cell aging and degenerative diseases caused by free radicals (highly reactive molecules within our bodies). The World Cancer Research Fund estimates that 40 per cent of cancers (approximately 4 million cases worldwide) can be avoided by following a healthy diet and not smoking.

do you need to lose weight?

Excessive weight gain is not inevitable as we age. In fact we should not weigh more than 9 kg/20 lbs more at the age of 50 than we did at 20, regardless of height. Many wieght charts are standardized to include age, height and sex; if your weight is 20 per cent above or below the standard, it is advisable to have a medical check up to ensure no problems exist.

In 1999, Dr Margaret Ashwell, a nutritionist, recommended a new and simple method of determining acceptable weight to the British Royal Society of Medicine. According to her method, if your waist measurement is less than half your height measurement, then your weight does not present a health hazard. If this method is applied to people in the UK, 15 per cent of men and 11 per cent of women can be considered dangerously overweight.

Another way of assessing weight is to calculate what percentage of your body consists of fat. This is a test that can be

▷ **Avoid elasticated waist bands on skirts and trousers since they allow clothes to remain comfortable, instead of giving early warning of creeping weight gain.**

◁ **White pasta offers less fibre, minerals and vitamins than wholemeal pasta, but is still a useful source of low-fat complex carbohydrate.**

performed by some health centres and sports clinics. On average our bodies are composed of approximately: 63 per cent water, 22 per cent protein, 13 per cent fat and 2 per cent vitamins and minerals.

If your fat ratio is significantly higher than 13 per cent a doctor is likely to advise you to reduce your fat intake and increase the amount of aerobic exercise you do. These are important measures in the prevention of chronic health problems.

As you get older it is advisable to avoid foods that contain too many additives such as sugar and salt, which are implicated in health problems such as hypertension and diabetes. As part of your dietary reassessment, study the labels of the foods in your kitchen. Compare the additives and ingredients in different foods. Ideally, the food on your shelves should be low in calories, saturated fat, sodium and sugar, and high in fibre and vitamins and minerals. If you become familiar with the composition of different foods, you will quickly become adept at monitoring what you are eating.

Throw away unhealthy recipes

When you are revising your eating habits, it can help to throw away recipes for unhealthy foods such as cakes, puddings and rich dishes that contain a lot of cream. This way you will not be tempted to cook them. Start to build a collection of new recipes that are low in fat and high in fibre, vitamins and minerals. Buy yourself a new cookery book containing healthy recipes.

▷ **Keep a variety of easy-to-prepare raw fruit and vegetables as nibbles, and only buy cakes and biscuits for special occasions.**

▽ **Try to make time to sit down and enjoy meals, rather than grabbing a quick snack on the run.**

How to eat a healthy diet

What we eat, and when, has a direct effect upon our body systems. By eating a balanced diet we can stay healthy, maintain energy levels, preserve healthy muscles and bones and help our brains to work efficiently, no matter how old we are. The guidelines for a balanced diet are straightforward and are based on eating the right amounts of foods from various different food groups.

- **Fats, oils and sugary foods:** 8 per cent
- **Meat, fish, eggs, nuts:** 14 per cent
- **Fruit and vegetables:** 34 per cent
- **Low-fat milk and dairy products:** 15 per cent
- **Bread, cereals and potatoes:** per cent

▷ **Once you know the ratio of different food types needed to maintain a healthy diet, planning meals becomes a lot easier.**

food groups

There is a broad consensus among doctors and nutritionists that foods fall into several discrete categories and that we should eat specific percentages of different types of foods. The breakdown of these food groups is shown in the pie chart above.

This breakdown exists as a rough guide and is not designed to be followed on a rigid daily basis. It does, however, show the emphasis that should be placed upon fruit, vegetables and complex carbohydrates.

when to eat

Traditionally, people have eaten three meals a day: breakfast in the morning, lunch at midday and dinner in the evening. Although this is a useful template, people often develop the habit of eating a small breakfast and lunch, and a large evening meal. This has a detrimental effect on digestion, especially as our digestive systems become more

sluggish with age. It also means that we have an inadequate supply of energy at the times of day when we are most active and a calorie overload at the end of the day when we are winding down.

A preferable eating pattern is a large breakfast, a substantial lunch and a comparatively small meal early in the evening. Alternatively, some people favour the grazing approach to eating in which they eat small quantities of food throughout the day. This prevents overloading the

△ **Allow yourself time to enjoy a healthy breakfast each morning.**

digestive system and ensures a consistent supply of energy throughout the day. The grazing method is also a good way of stabilizing blood sugar levels in the body, which may be useful for people suffering from adult-onset diabetes.

how healthy is meat?

Meat has had a lot of bad press in many countries in recent years for reasons such as infection with bovine spongiform encephalopathy (BSE) or the presence of antibiotics. Meat is high in saturated fat, which is implicated in the development of heart disease. It is also high in an amino acid called arachidonic acid, which increases levels of pro-inflammatory chemicals and should therefore be avoided by people of a rheumatic disposition. It does, however, still remain possible to eat meat safely. If you are concerned about the presence of antibiotics, choose organically produced meat, and cut away any visible fat on meat to avoid consuming too much saturated fat. Moderation is the key: the World Cancer Research Fund recommends that no more than 75g/3oz of meat should be eaten per day.

Eaten in moderation, meat is a useful source of antioxidant minerals such as zinc and selenium. Antioxidants can help prevent degenerative diseases, such as cancer. Beef is a good source of iron, zinc and B vitamins; choose lean cuts such as topside in which the fat content is only 2.7 per cent per 115g/4oz – minced beef can contain up to 25 per cent fat.

Pork supplies B vitamins, iron, zinc and selenium. Excess fat should be removed, and pork crackling should be avoided. Chicken supplies only about half the zinc and iron of red meats, but if the skin is removed prior to cooking it is very low in fat. It is also an excellent source of the antioxidant selenium.

Older people are advised to eat plenty of oily fish because they contain omega-3 fatty acids. These are essential fatty acids that are vital for health but cannot be made by the body. Omega-3 fatty acids can help to fight against heart disease, and are found in abundance in salmon, mackerel, sardines, pilchards, herrings, kippers and tuna.

◁ Buying small, easy-to-prepare cuts of meat will help you to monitor the amount of saturated fat that you eat each day.

▽ Instead of using heavy, fattening sauces to liven up fish, try sprinkling it with herbs to help bring out the full flavour.

Anti-aging foods

The general guidelines for the anti-aging diet are: keep your calorie consumption and saturated fat intake down; eat plenty of wholegrains, oily fish and fresh fruit and vegetables; and cut down on salt and sugar. In addition to these general guidelines, there are specific foods that have a role in anti-aging and that you should regularly include in your diet.

△ An avocado a is very versatile fruit that can be eaten either cooked or raw, and used in both savoury and sweet dishes.

avocado

This fruit, which is usually eaten as a vegetable, is a good source of healthy monounsaturated fat that may help to reduce levels of a bad type of cholesterol in the body. Avocado is a good source of vitamin E and can help to maintain healthy skin and prevent skin aging (vitamin E may also help alleviate menopausal hot flushes). It is rich in potassium which helps prevent fluid retention and high blood pressure.

berries

All black and blue berries such as blackberries, blueberries, blackcurrants and black grapes contain phytochemicals known as flavonoids – powerful antioxidants which help to protect the body against damage caused by free radicals and aging.

cruciferous vegetables

The family of cruciferous vegetables includes cabbage, cauliflower, broccoli, kale, turnip, brussels sprouts, radish and watercress. Cruciferous vegetables assist the body in its fight against toxins and cancer. You should try to consume at least 115g/4oz (of any one or a combination) of these vegetables on a daily basis. If possible, eat them raw or very lightly cooked so that the important enzymes remain intact.

△ Blueberries are rich in vitamin C and flavonoids which help to prevent cancer.

▽ Broccoli, cabbage and cauliflower contain high levels of cancer-fighting phytochemicals.

△ You can boost your garlic consumption by taking it as a supplement.

△ Rice and pasta are good low-fat carbohydrates.

garlic

Eating a clove of garlic a day (raw or cooked) helps to protect the body against cancer and heart disease. The cardioprotective effects of garlic are well recorded. One 1994 study in Iowa, USA, of 41,837 women between the ages of 55 and 69 suggested that women who ate a clove of garlic at least once a week were 50 per cent less likely to develop colon cancer. Another study at Tasgore Medical College in India suggested that garlic reduced cholesterol levels and assisted blood thinning more effectively than aspirin, thus helping to reduce the risk of heart disease.

ginger

This spicy root can boost the digestive and circulatory systems, which can be useful for older people. Ginger may also help to alleviate rheumatic aches and pains.

▽ A glass of hot water with a little ginger can alleviate nausea, especially car and sea sickness.

nuts

Most varieties of nuts are good sources of minerals, particularly walnuts and brazil nuts. Walnuts, although high in calories, are rich in potassium, magnesium, iron, zinc, copper and selenium. Adding nuts to your diet (sprinkle them on salads and desserts) can enhance the functioning of your digestive and immune systems, improve your skin and help prevent cancer. Nuts may also help control cholesterol levels. Never eat rancid nuts, however, as they have been linked to a high incidence of free radicals.

△ Brazil nuts are rich in magnesium and selenium.

soya

Menopausal women might find that soya helps to maintain oestrogen levels. Soya may alleviate menopausal hot flushes and protect against Alzheimer's disease, osteoporosis and heart disease. Look out for fermented soya products, which are more easily digested, therefore more nutritional, and do not generally cause food intolerances. You may want to check that soya products have not been genetically modified. Soya should not be confused with soy sauce, which is full of salt and should be used sparingly, if at all.

▷ Chilled water melon is refreshing on hot days.

wholemeal pasta and rice

Complex carbohydrates provide a consistent supply of energy throughout the day and should make up the bulk of your diet. Wholemeal pasta is an excellent complex carbohydrate. It is high in fibre and contains twice the amount of iron as normal pasta. Brown rice is another recommended complex carbohydrate, which is high in fibre and B vitamins.

watermelon

Both the flesh and seeds of the watermelon are nutritious so try blending them together in a food processor and drinking as a juice. The flesh contains vitamins A, B and C; the seeds contain selenium, essential fats, zinc and vitamin E, all of which help against free radical damage and aging.

Food intolerance

Many people find that they start to suffer from food intolerance as they grow older. This is partly due to long-term exposure to an irritating substance and partly due to the fact that the digestive system becomes less efficient with age. Eating foods to which you are intolerant is like continually stubbing your toe – the discomfort will become worse over a period of time and eventually the damage can become permanent.

what is food intolerance?

A food intolerance should not be confused with an allergy. An intolerance occurs when the body finds a substance difficult to cope with, whereas an allergy to a substance is an active fight that involves the body's immune system.

Although there are many different types of food intolerance, some foods are more likely to cause intolerances than others. They include soya products, caffeine, chocolate, orange juice, tomatoes and food additives. Two foods that commonly cause intolerances are cow's milk and wheat (or other grains).

If you have an intolerance to cow's milk, this means that your body finds it difficult to digest lactose, the sugar found in milk. As a result, lactose moves through the

△ Tomatoes are a good source of disease-fighting antioxidants, but some people may find they develop an intolerance to them.

◁ By keeping a diary of foods ingested each day, it is often possible to detect small intolerances before they become too problematic.

intestines undigested and when it reaches the colon, bacteria start to ferment it, producing gas. The result may be abdominal discomfort, flatulence and diarrhoea.

An intolerance to wheat and grains means that you have difficulty digesting the protein gluten. Gluten intolerance can cause weight loss, loss of appetite, abdominal cramps and poor vitamin and mineral absorption from food.

detecting food intolerances

You may already suspect that you have an intolerance to a particular food, simply because you suffer discomfort when you consume it. To confirm that this is the case, try eliminating the suspicious food for a month before re-introducing it to your diet. Keep a daily diary of your symptoms and note whether they return when you re-introduce the food. Alternatively, you can seek the professional advice of a doctor, dietician or naturopath.

▷ Soya milk offers a good alternative to dairy products containing lactose. Although soya beans have a higher fat content than other pulses, the fat is mostly unsaturated and is considered to be non-harmful.

dealing with food intolerances

There is no cure for food intolerance except simply avoiding the relevant foods. If you identify the foods that you cannot tolerate, you can look for alternatives that satisfy your nutritional needs and personal tastes. For example, if you cannot tolerate orange juice, drink

Signs to look out for

You may have a food intolerance if you suffer from any of the following symptoms on a regular basis:

- Anxiety
- Depression
- Fatigue
- Headaches
- Skin disorders
- Asthma
- Joint or muscle pain
- Rheumatoid arthritis
- Ulcers (mouth or stomach)
- Water retention
- Stomach bloating
- Nausea
- Vomiting
- Constipation
- Diarrhoea
- Irritable bowel syndrome

▽ For those suffering from lactose intolerance, live yogurt is easier to digest than milk, and is a good way to boost calcium levels.

△ Corn is a good alternative to wheat for those with a gluten intolerance.

apple juice instead. It may not even be necessary to exclude foods completely. For example, if you have an intolerance to cow's milk you may still be able to tolerate a small amount of milk in one cup of tea a day.

If you are lactose intolerant try to avoid dairy products, and check food labels for the presence of lactose. Substitute soya milk for cow's milk. Women who need to exclude dairy products should ensure that they receive enough calcium from other sources to maintain healthy bones. Live yogurt is a good calcium source for people who are lactose intolerant (the bacteria present in the yogurt helps to break down lactose). Gluten intolerant people should avoid wheat, rye, and barley. Switching to corn, rice, soya, and potato starch can be helpful.

Warning

If you are suffering from unusual digestive complaints such as nausea, diarrhoea or persistent indigestion, seek a diagnosis from your doctor before you make any dietary changes. A full elimination diet should be supervised by a medical professional.

Dietary tips

Nutritionists and dietary therapists have now identified the eating habits that bring health and those that do not. The main guideline for a healthy diet as we grow older is to eat a diet rich in antioxidants – substances that actively fight the cell damage that leads to aging. Antioxidants are found in abundance in fruit and vegetables. There are a number of other guidelines that become especially important with age.

good and bad fats

Some fats are necessary for health and others are harmful. Unsaturated fats are essential to our bodies for the transportation of vitamins A, D, E and K, lowering harmful cholesterol, and aiding the nervous system, cardiovascular system and brain. Good sources of unsaturated fat are olive oil, oily fish, nuts and seeds.

Saturated fats are linked to the build up of fatty deposits on artery walls leading to blocked arteries. There may also be an association between high saturated fat intake and certain cancers. Foods that contain saturated fat should be avoided or eaten in moderation. They include meat,

△ **Stir frying is a quick and easy way to prepare appetizing low-fat meals.**

dairy products and palm and coconut oils. Fried food and fat found in cakes, cookies and prepared meals should also be avoided.

▷ **Sunflower seeds are a good source of vitamin B₃ (niacin) which can fight against depression, circulatory problems, high blood pressure and cholesterol, tinnitus, and breathing problems in asthmatics.**

Avoiding fats
- Check food labels for hidden fats.
- Choose low-fat cooking techniques, such as grilling or stir-frying.
- When cooking meat, place it on a rack so that excess fat drips off.
- Add yogurt rather than cream to your desserts.
- Buy canned fish in brine rather than in oil.

understanding cholesterol

Not all cholesterol is unhealthy. There are two types of cholesterol: high density lipoprotein (HDL) which is popularly known as "good cholesterol", and low density lipoprotein (LDL), popularly known as "bad cholesterol".

Explained simply, HDL stops the build up of fatty deposits in the arteries and LDL creates them. If your HDL levels are high compared to your LDL levels, then you are at a low risk of cardiovascular disease. The ideal ratio is thought to be three parts HDL to one part LDL.

As you age it is important to maximize your cardiovascular health by keeping your LDL levels low and your HDL levels high. The best way to achieve this is to avoid fried foods and saturated and hydrogenated fats – the main sources of LDL. (Hydrogenation is a process that turns vegetable oil into hard fat.) Other ways to promote a healthy HDL/LDL balance include:
- eating plenty of garlic
- a diet rich in vitamin C
- eating foods rich in vitamin B₃
- including plenty of oily fish in your diet

cut out sugar and salt

Although complex carbohydrates, such as whole grains and pulses, are good for us, simple carbohydrates such as refined sugar are not. All forms of sugar whether brown sugar, white sugar, honey or syrup cause our blood sugar levels to increase rapidly. If this instant supply of energy is not used, the body stores it and eventually it is converted into fat. Keep refined sugar intake to a minimum; it has no nutritional value and causes sudden highs in blood sugar levels, followed by slumps that can leave you feeling moody and irritable. If you have a sugar craving, eat a piece of fruit. Sugar, and the foods that it is found in (candy, cakes and many other processed foods), are said to contain "empty calories" because they offer short-lived energy without the benefit of nutrients such as vitamins and minerals.

Cut down on salt or eliminate it from your diet and never eat more than about a teaspoon a day. Too much salt causes fluid retention, places stress on the kidneys and heart, and lessens the amount of potassium absorbed by the body. High blood pressure becomes more likely as we get older, and a high-salt diet can contribute to its development. Check for the presence of salt or sodium chloride on food labels, and where possible avoid adding salt to food during cooking or at the dining table.

fibre – nature's broom

Dietary fibre is essential for a healthy digestive system. It is sometimes referred to as "nature's broom" because it sweeps

△ The membranes around orange segments contain a soluble fibre, pectin, which helps to lower levels of LDL cholesterol. Oranges also contain vitamin C and flavonoids, which maintain healthy skin and help in the fight against disease.

through the intestines transporting debris and residue out of the body. Fibre is not digested by the body so it retains its original mass and contributes to healthy, regular bowel movements. It may also decrease the amount of fat absorbed by the body and help to protect the arteries. Fibre absorbs water in the intestines so it is important to drink extra water if you include a lot of fibre in your diet. Try to eat plenty of natural sources of fibre such as lentils, dried beans, seeds, whole grains, fruit and vegetables.

be sparing with protein

Protein is essential for life, but only a very small amount is needed each day. Too much can contribute to a variety of health problems, including osteoporosis. Most of us eat far more protein than we actually need and, contrary to popular belief, many plant foods are rich in protein. For example, a meal containing rice and lentils, but no meat or dairy products, is a source of good quality protein. Estimates for protein requirement vary, but range from 4.5 to 8 per cent of our total calorie intake. Try to eat less protein foods and replace animal proteins with plant proteins, such as tofu, spinach and pumpkin seeds. Plant proteins are advantageous in that they contain fibre but no saturated fat.

▽ Beans offer a good source of low-fat fibre and are cholesterol free and high in protein, iron and B vitamins.

▽ Tofu is made from soya beans and is a valuable addition to vegan and dairy-free diets.

Drinking fluids

Water is a vital nutrient and one that we cannot store in the body. We lose water all the time through sweat, urination, defecation and simply exhaling water vapour. It is essential to drink a minimum of 1.5 litres/2½ pints of water a day, preferably 2 litres/3½ pints. As we grow older our thirst mechanism becomes less reliable and we are more prone to dehydration.

water – the healthiest drink

The best drink to keep the body hydrated is pure water. Fruit and vegetable juice and herbal teas are also good choices. Soft drinks that contain flavouring, preservatives and sugar can place stress on the body or add "empty calories" to your diet and should be drunk infrequently. If your diet is very high in fibre, you will need to drink extra water (fibre absorbs water in the intestines).

Carbonated water is an acceptable alternative to still water, but it should be drunk in moderation, as dietary therapists believe it raises the pH of the stomach and the reduced acidity makes it harder for the body to digest protein.

△ A glass of body-temperature water with a slice of lemon is a good drink to wake up the body each morning.

▽ Carrot juice is a tasty source of vitamin A, which fights against cancer and heart disease.

Apart from preventing dehydration, keeping up your fluid intake may help to prevent bladder cancer as you get older. This may be because a regular flow of fluid prevents prolonged exposure of the bladder tissue to potential carcinogens. Drinking water is also good for your appearance: if your skin is properly hydrated it will look younger and healthier.

don't rely on thirst

As you grow older you should not rely on feeling thirsty to tell you when to drink. Instead, drink water throughout the day and monitor the colour of your urine. A pale golden colour means that you are probably getting enough to drink; dark amber means that you are not. Dehydration can be exacerbated by hot climates, exercise, alcohol, illness (especially vomiting and diarrhoea) and taking diuretic medications.

Most people do not drink enough fluid on a daily basis to keep the body fully hydrated, or they drink too many diuretic drinks, such as coffee, which increase the body's fluid loss. As a result, many of us suffer from symptoms of mild dehydration such as fatigue and headaches, and the body functions at a sub-optimum level. If you become seriously dehydrated, your skin becomes dry, your eyes appear sunken, your urine turns dark and you may suffer from constipation, dizziness, nausea, cramps, confusion, low blood pressure and itchiness.

△ The flavonoids in red grape skins are thought to reduce arterial and immune system aging.

alcohol

As you get older, alcohol can take its toll on the body. Drinking more than recommended guidelines places stress on the liver, hinders the absorption of nutrients, dehydrates the body, damages cells and causes the body to age prematurely. This is especially noticeable in the skin. Yet if alcohol is drunk in moderation, it can offer some benefits. Half to one unit per day for women and two units for men may help to reduce arterial aging and heart attacks. Scientists are not entirely certain how alcohol produces these beneficial effects, but some believe that it may prevent fat from oxidizing and forming deposits on artery walls.

Red wine may be beneficial if drunk in moderation. The flavonoids in red grape skins are thought to have antioxidant properties. Antioxidants help to prevent disease and the degeneration of body cells.

caffeinated drinks

Some of our most popular drinks, such as tea, coffee and cola drinks, contain caffeine. Apart from its diuretic effect, opinions are mixed about whether caffeine constitutes a threat to health. It is therefore advisable to drink caffeinated drinks in moderation (no more than 2 or 3 cups a day). Overuse may cause sleep disturbances, prevent vitamins and minerals from being used effectively by the body, raise blood pressure and cause an increase in the secretion of stress hormones. Different types of coffee contain different amounts of caffeine: instant coffee contains the least caffeine; ground, unfiltered coffee contains the most. A good alternative is steamed decaffeinated coffee, which unlike other decaffeination processes, does not involve the addition of toxic chemicals. For a healthier alternative try dandelion coffee or a cereal beverage made with barley or chicory.

How to stay hydrated

- Eat foods with a high water content such as fruit and soup.
- Drink a glass of water as soon as you get up in the morning.
- Drink a glass of water at least half-an-hour before each meal.
- Sip water at 10 to 15-minute intervals during exercise (many people underestimate how much they sweat; try weighing yourself before and after you sweat).
- Drink water at the first sign of a headache or muscle cramp.
- Choose low-caffeine or decaffeinated drinks that will not have a diuretic effect on the body.
- Buy a juicer and make your own fruit and vegetable juices. Alternatively, make fruit smoothies in a blender.

∧ Keeping the body hydrated helps to cleanse the body by ensuring the elimination of toxins.

herbal teas

A great variety of herbal teas are available, and you can even make your own herbal infusions with medicinal benefits. Herbal teas have the benefit of hydrating the body while being caffeine free. To make a cup of camomile tea, place a handful of the fresh herb in a teapot, pour on boiling water, leave to infuse for 5 minutes, stir and pour through a strainer. Camomile can help to relieve anxiety and insomnia.

▷ Readily available and easily prepared, mint tea is a good remedy for nausea, migraine, indigestion, flatulence, and irritable bowel syndrome.

Weight loss

△ **A healthy alternative to oil-based salad dressings is to squeeze fresh lemon juice onto the salad immediately before serving.**

As you grow older, being overweight puts you at risk of a range of health problems including diabetes and hypertension. If you are overweight, changing your diet can significantly reduce your chances of illness (as well as raise your self-esteem). You do not have to go on a starvation diet to lose weight, but you do need to make long-term changes to your eating patterns by cutting out processed foods and full-fat products.

consume fewer calories

The rate at which you burn energy or calories – your metabolic rate – slows down as you get older (a calorie is the amount of heat needed to raise the temperature of 1 litre/ $1^{3}/_{4}$ pints of water by one degree). You may find that continuing to eat the same amount that you did previously causes you to slowly gain weight. The way to lose weight is to consume fewer calories than you expend so that the body is forced to burn stored fat.

Daily calorie requirements vary according to your lifestyle, but, as a rough guide, women need approximately 2,000 calories per day and men need 2,500. These figures increase if you have an active lifestyle. By eating 1,000 calories less than these energy requirements each day, you should be able to achieve a steady weight loss of about $1kg/2^{1}/_{4}$ lbs a week, although the loss may be higher at first due to fluid losses. It is not advisable to lose more than $1kg/2^{1}/_{4}$ lbs a week as you are likely to be losing fluid, and bone and muscle mass, all of which can accelerate the aging process.

Many foods are labelled with their calorie contents, so it is easy to become familiar with the energy values of different foods. You should, however, try not to count calories obsessively.

types of food

The types of food that you should eat during a weight-loss diet are the same as those for a normal, well-balanced diet: concentrate on complex carbohydrates and fresh fruit and vegetables. Avoid fatty foods especially saturated fats (found in meat, dairy products

▽ **Always strain herbal teas prior to drinking to allow the subtle fragrance and flavour through without any bitter aftertaste from the leaves.**

△ **Rest a slice of lemon in a glass of boiling water for five minutes for a refreshing drink to enjoy at any time of day.**

and coconut and palm oils). Remember that fats contain twice as many calories as carbohydrates and proteins:

    1g carbohydrate = 4 calories
    1g protein = 4 calories
    1g fat = 9 calories

As well as eating low-fat foods, try to eat little and often. Start the day with a glass of warm (body temperature) water and a slice of lemon. Eat a breakfast of wholegrains – such as wholemeal toast or muesli – half an hour after getting up. Avoid butter and use skimmed instead of full-fat milk. Snack on raw vegetables until lunch time and then make lunch the main meal of the day. Drink fruit juices, smoothies made with low-fat yogurt and herbal teas in the afternoon. Try to eat a light dinner a minimum of 3 hours before going to bed. Eat raw fruit whenever you feel hungry. Keep meals under 350 calories and allow 250 calories for drinks and snacks such as apples and carrots.

tips for losing weight

Before starting to diet, set yourself a target weight. If you are particularly overweight, you may want to decide this in conjunction

△ **Many people find exercise easier to maintain if they undertake it as a routine social interaction, such as jogging with a partner each day, or exercising the dog.**

◁ **Fluid, longline clothing is more slimming than clothing that cuts the body in half or is more bulky.**

with your doctor. If you are only slightly overweight, you may simply want to slim down until you can fit into a favourite item of clothing. If you have a lapse in your diet, do not see it as a reason to give up. Remember that you are only human.

Avoid alcohol: not only is it high in calories, but research in Holland has found that people who drank alcohol half an hour before a meal ate quicker and consumed more calories than those who remained alcohol free. Instead, drink a glass of water before a meal to help you feel full.

Avoid using dieting aids or diuretics to assist weight loss, since they will upset the body's natural balance, and can lead to problems such as vitamin deficiencies and digestive disorders.

Combine your weight-loss diet with regular aerobic exercise. This will help to speed up fat loss and develop firm muscles.

When you have reached your target weight, continue to eat sensibly. Try to keep meals to fewer than 500 calories so the body can break down each meal easily. This allows three meals of 500 calories as well as drinks and snacks of fruit.

Dietary supplements

Although the diet can provide many essential nutrients as you grow older, there are some vitamins and minerals that you may need to take in supplement form. Some dietary therapists say that the modern Western diet and lifestyle exposes people to so many nutrient "depleters" that supplements are the best way to achieve optimum nutrition.

your nutrient needs

Deficiency in fat, carbohydrate or protein is very rare in the West, but experts believe that many of us are lacking in vitamins and minerals. However, it is difficult to work out exactly which vitamins and minerals you receive in abundance and those that you may need to supplement. The best advice is to consult a naturopath or dietician who will carry out a detailed analysis of your personal nutritional needs. Both your hair and blood can be analyzed to provide information about the nutritional state of your body.

Even without professional assessment, you can make a reasonable estimate of your needs by looking at the foods you eat in your diet and examining your lifestyle and current health. For example, if your diet includes many substances, such as salt, sugar, caffeine and alcohol, that deplete the body of nutrients, then it may be advisable to take a

△ **Supplements come in many forms; chelated supplements, however, contain amino acids which make them more readily absorbed by the body for maximum benefit.**

multivitamin and mineral supplement. Diet can sometimes be misleading though; you may eat healthy foods but still have problems absorbing all the nutrients you need for health.

If you have a stressful lifestyle, smoke cigarettes, drink alcohol and are exposed to environmental pollution on a daily basis, then you are very unlikely to be getting all the vitamins and minerals that you need. If this is the case, taking daily supplements is probably advisable.

Your current health is often a good indication of whether you are suffering from sub-optimum nutrition or deficiency. Problems as diverse as mouth ulcers, muscle cramps, frequent colds, irritability and dry skin can often – but not always – be traced to a lack of essential vitamins and minerals.

Daily nutrient intake

Recommended daily allowances (RDAs) are standard amounts set by governments. They represent the daily amounts of a nutrient that we should consume in order to stay healthy. RDAs are criticized by some dietary therapists who say that they are far too low. It is argued that, although an RDA is high enough to prevent a deficiency disease such as scurvy (caused by insufficient vitamin C), it is not high enough to keep the body functioning at an optimum level for health and wellbeing. Critics say that RDAs should be increased to encourage people to eat healthier diets.

◁ **Many health problems can reduce the body's ability to absorb nutrients, and it may be worth visiting a nutritionist who can advise on your dietary requirements.**

△ Effervescent vitamin C tablets are pleasant to take, but many of them contain artificial sweeteners and flavourings.

what are supplements?

Supplements usually come in tablet form. They contain a stated amount of the essential nutrient plus other ingredients, such as fillers, bindings and coatings to give bulk, consistency and shape to the tablet. If you cannot tolerate cow's milk, check that supplements are lactose-free. Follow the instructions regarding dosage carefully.

Some supplements (usually vitamin C and B vitamins) work on a slow release basis because they cannot be stored efficiently by the body. To avoid the product being excreted, slow release systems gradually release the nutrients, usually over a period of six hours, to allow maximum benefit.

Liquid supplements often contain sugars and sweeteners, but are easily assimilated into the body. Always take a liquid supplement in the dosage stated and do not drink it directly from the bottle or guess the amount taken.

which supplements?

Some health problems become more common with age and they can be prevented or alleviated with supplements. Consult a nutritionist or dietary therapist if you are in any doubt which supplement to take in which dosage.

- General prevention of aging and degenerative diseases: vitamin A, C, E, betacarotene, selenium, zinc or a general antioxidant supplement.

△ Tinctures should be dropped directly onto, or underneath, the tongue for easy absorption.

- Menopausal symptoms: evening primrose oil, vitamin C with bioflavonoids, vitamin E, or a general multivitamin and mineral supplement.
- Prostate problems: saw palmetto (for enlarged prostate), general antioxidant supplement, or a general multivitamin and mineral supplement.
- Osteoporosis: bone mineral complex, vitamin C, or a general multivitamin and mineral supplement.
- High blood pressure: vitamin C, general antioxidant, or a general multivitamin and mineral supplement.
- Diabetes: vitamin C, B complex, zinc, chromium, or a general multivitamin and mineral supplement.
- Arthritis: vitamin C, vitamin B5, gamma-linolenic acid (GLA), eicosapentaenoic acid (EPA), bone mineral complex, general antioxidant supplement, or a general multivitamin and mineral supplement.

▽ Gelatine capsules are unsuitable for vegetarians and vegans, who should look for seaweed alternatives.

Staying fit throughout life

In conjunction with a healthy diet, exercise is the best way to stay well, slow down the aging process and keep your body fit, toned, agile and attractive. You can reap huge benefits from relatively small increases in your activity levels. For example, walking instead of driving, swimming once or twice a week and doing some weight–lifting exercises in front of the television will quickly increase your overall fitness levels. You are never too old to start exercising.

Taking up exercise

Exercise is a vital part of preventative health care as you get older. By taking regular exercise you can prevent weight gain and keep all your organs and body systems healthy. You will also help to prevent cardiovascular disease, osteoporosis, arthritis and many other health problems.

△ T'ai chi is a non-combative martial art reputedly practised by Taoist monks in 13th-century China. It uses fluid, graceful sequences along with controlled breathing to exercise the body, calm the mind and promote self healing.

the effects of exercise

The heart is a muscle and needs to be exercised just like any other muscle in order to stay strong and healthy. Working the heart during exercise also maintains the health of the arteries and ensures that blood circulates to all the body's organs, keeping them supplied with oxygen and nutrients.

Exercise has a beneficial effect on every part of the body. It keeps the skin and hair in good condition, it makes you more energetic, it speeds up the passage of food through the digestive system, it speeds up metabolism (the rate at which the body

Staying motivated

Enthusiasm and motivation may be high at the beginning of a new exercise campaign but typically wane as the weeks go by.

- Try to make exercising part of your normal everyday routine, like combing your hair or eating dinner.
- Make exercise sociable and enjoyable: exercise with a friend or in a group.
- Choose an exercise that's right for you. If you find the gym boring, try other forms of exercise: join an exercise class, play tennis or squash or go swimming.
- A sense of achievement can act as a motivating force. Whenever you reach a target, however small, set yourself a new one.
- Fit exercise into your day. If you are very busy, find opportunities for exercise in your existing schedule. For example, cycle to work, take the stairs instead of the elevator or use a manual lawnmower to mow the grass.
- Keep reminding yourself of the health benefits of exercise and the dangers of a sedentary life. Exercise is an investment in your current and future health.

△ Touching your toes is a good way to improve flexibility in the hips and spine.

burns calories), it strengthens bones and muscles, it stabilizes blood sugar, it prevents weight gain and, if you are carrying surplus fat, it helps you to shed it. In other words, exercise prevents many of the physical changes that come with age. Exercise also has a positive effect on the mind and

△ Gardening is a great way to keep your body in good shape while enjoying the outdoors.

emotions. It is an excellent way of alleviating stress, beating depression and raising your self-esteem.

how fit are you?

Your resting heart rate provides a rough guide to your overall level of fitness. Generally, the lower your heart rate, the fitter you are. If you know that you are very unfit, you have not exercised for many years, you are overweight or you have health problems, you should consult your doctor before taking up exercise. To measure your heart rate, press your first two fingers

Fitness levels indicated by heart beats per minute

MEN

Age 20–29
Very fit: less than 60
Fit: 60–69
Moderate: 70–85
Unfit: over 85

Age 30–39
Very fit: less than 64
Fit: 64–71
Moderate: 72–85
Unfit: over 85

Age 40–49
Very fit: less than 65
Fit: 65–73
Moderate: 74–90
Unfit: over 90

Age 50 +
Very fit: less than 68
Fit: 68–75
Moderate: 76–90
Unfit: over 90

WOMEN

Age 20–29
Very fit: less than 72
Fit: 72–77
Moderate: 78–95
Unfit: over 95

Age 30–39
Very fit: less than 72
Fit: 72–79
Moderate: 80–97
Unfit: over 97

Age 40–49
Very fit: less than 75
Fit: 75–79
Moderate: 80–98
Unfit: over 98

Age 50+
Very fit: less than 75
Fit: 75–85
Moderate: 85–102
Unfit: over 102

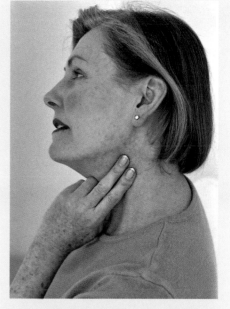

△ **To calculate your pulse rate place the tips of your first two fingers on the pulse point at the side of your neck or on your inner wrist.**

lightly on the pulse point in your neck and count the number of beats over a 15 second period, then multiply that number by 4 to calculate the number of beats per minute.

how hard should I exercise?

While you are exercising, your optimum heart rate should always be between 60 and 80 per cent of the maximum heart rate (MHR) for your age. In order to calculate your MHR, you simply subtract your age from 220.

220–age = MHR

Next you should calculate 60 per cent of your MHR. This is the minimum elevation of your heart rate that you should aim for during exercise. Then calculate 80 per cent of your MHR. This is the maximum elevation of your heart rate that you should aim for during exercise. A heart rate that is between 60 per cent and 80 per cent of your MHR is said to be in your "training zone". If you are 50 years old, your MHR is 170, your minimum training heart rate is 102 and your maximum training heart rate is 136. If you stick to these guidelines, you will be able to burn body fat and exercise your cardiovascular system safely.

When you have finished exercising, you should check that your heart returns to its normal rate within 10 minutes. If it takes

◁ **Once you become more agile through exercise you could try out an adventurous new sport.**

longer than 10 minutes, it is advisable that you exercise at a slower pace until you become fitter. Another quick test to ascertain whether you are exerting yourself too hard is known as the "talking test". Make sure that you can always hold a conversation while you are exercising. If you find that you are too out of breath or fatigued to talk, then you are probably exercising too hard.

▽ **Yoga tones muscles and stretches the spine.**

Aerobic exercise

There are three broad categories of exercise: aerobic exercise, anaerobic exercise and flexibility exercise. These are also known as the three "Ss": stamina, strength and suppleness. As you grow older, your heart needs a regular aerobic workout to function efficiently, your muscles need strength training to prevent them from losing mass, and your joints need flexibility exercise to maintain a full range of movement.

aerobic exercise

Aerobic exercises are those which bring your heart rate into the "training zone" (60 to 80 per cent of your maximum heart rate) and increase the body's circulation and respiratory rate. Aerobic exercise is sustained by oxygen and it is sometimes called fat-burning exercise, cardiovascular exercise or cardiowork. Aerobic exercise can be kept up for long periods of time; in fact the longer you exercise for, the more calories you burn up and the greater the health benefits.

benefits of aerobic exercise

Aerobic exercise gives the heart a good workout, burns up fat, boosts the immune system and helps to prevent the build-up of fatty deposits in the arteries. It enhances joint and muscle flexibility, stamina, sleep and digestion, and it normalizes hormone levels, helping to alleviate premenstrual syndrome and menopausal symptoms. Aerobic exercise that is also weight-bearing can help to prevent osteoporosis by strengthening and slowing down the loss of calcium in the bones.

◁ For those without joint problems, cycling provides an enjoyable form of aerobic exercise as well as a pollutant-free form of transport.

△ The most commonly used form of t'ai chi used in the West is Yang, a slow series of postures performed as a flowing exercise routine.

types of aerobic exercise

Walking, jogging, cycling, swimming and dancing are effective, cheap and fun ways of taking aerobic exercise. Most gyms hold a range of classes that teach aerobic routines. Some classes use steps and weights, some are high impact and others are low impact – choose a class that matches your fitness level.

Swimming is not a weight-bearing exercise and should be combined with another form of exercise, such as walking, in order to preserve healthy bones.

getting started

Aerobic exercise can put stress on the heart if you are not accustomed to it and this is especially true for older people or those who are overweight. For this reason, it is essential to start slowly and build up gradually. As the fitness level of the body increases, the heart will slowly gain strength, until it reaches a point at which it does not need to work so hard to supply the body with sufficient oxygen to maintain exercise.

At this point you will have made a positive change to your fitness levels and should start feeling the benefits of exercise.

Walking is a good way to get started on a programme of aerobic exercise: try walking to work or to the shops and walking upstairs whenever possible. As you become fitter, increase the challenge by walking faster and for longer periods, or try hill-walking. You can also join a low-impact aerobic class and work at your own pace. Cardiovascular equipment in gyms – such as treadmills and training bikes – is useful because it provides immediate feedback on your heart rate, allowing you to slow down if you are working too hard. Alternatively, you can buy a heart rate monitor for this purpose.

Once you have reached a reasonable level of fitness, try to do at least 35 minutes of aerobic exercise (excluding warming up and cooling down) three or four times a week.

△ **Walking helps to stabilize blood sugar levels, thus regulating mood swings and energy levels, as well as fighting osteoporosis, weight gain, and heart disease.**

▷ **A rowing machine can help to strengthen the spine and muscular system, but for those with back problems should only be used under supervision.**

Guidelines for exercising

- Stop exercising at any time if you feel dizzy, faint, nauseous or in pain.
- Always warm up and cool down before and after exercise to allow a slow build up to your training zone heart rate and to avoid injury to muscles, tendons and ligaments.
- If you lift weights, do not train the same muscle groups on consecutive days. Allow at least one or two days of rest between training sessions.
- Always pay careful attention to your posture when lifting weights.
- Try to take moderate exercise three or four times a week rather than intensive exercise intermittently.
- If possible, get a personally tailored exercise programme from a doctor, fitness instructor or personal trainer.
- Always wear comfortable, well-fitting sneakers that cushion the feet and offer good ankle support.
- When swimming, avoid the breast stroke if you suffer from back problems.
- Take care when exercising outside. Try to avoid exercising in adverse weather conditions and do not exercise in deserted places. Wear sufficient layers (you can shed them if you need to) and make sure that you are visible to traffic.

Anaerobic exercise

The term "anaerobic" means "without oxygen". During anaerobic exercise, muscles work at high intensity for a short period of time. Whereas oxygen enables long periods of exercise, anaerobic exercise is necessarily short in duration.

Anaerobic exercise results in the build up of a by-product known as lactic acid in the muscles. This causes discomfort and fatigue, which is another reason why anaerobic exercise cannot be sustained over long periods of time. Lactic acid must leave the muscles before you can attempt further anaerobic exercise.

benefits of taking anaerobic exercise

Anaerobic exercise has far-reaching benefits for your body and health. It will keep your muscles strong and prepare your body for quick bursts of activity, such as running to catch a train or fleeing from danger. Strong, toned muscles have a variety of health benefits. They improve your posture, they give the body a lean and taut appearance, they make you physically stronger and more powerful, and the more muscle tissue you build up, the more calories you will burn off, even during periods of inactivity. You lose muscle tissue as you age (up to a third by the age of 65). In fact, a significant cause of low energy levels, fatigue and immobility in middle and later life is the decline in the amount of skeletal muscle. You can reverse this by taking anaerobic exercise several times a week.

types of anaerobic exercise

Examples of anaerobic exercise include weight lifting, sprinting, or any rapid burst of hard exercise. For example, squash is an anaerobic form of exercise because it involves short and intensive movements. Some types of yoga are anaerobic, for example, postures that involve taking your own body weight on your hands.

getting started

There are several ways to get started on a regular programme of anaerobic exercise. Some people join a gym and use the weights and resistance machines; others take up swimming, squash or yoga. However, the easiest (and cheapest) way to get started is to lift some weights at home.

Instead of spending money on weights, fill two plastic water bottles with rice. Using this method you can adjust the weight whenever you need to. Remember, your first aim is to tone muscles, not increase their bulk. Start by lifting a small weight a few times and increase the weight and the number of repetitions when the exercises become easier.

You can also strengthen the muscles without using weights. The simplest muscle exercises involve repeatedly clenching and relaxing muscles. This works best on muscles such as the buttocks that are easy to isolate. It is also the principle underlying Kegel exercises which strengthen the pubococcygeal muscles and help to support the pelvic organs. To practise Kegel exercises, simply contract the pelvic floor muscles, hold for 5 seconds and release. Repeat three times.

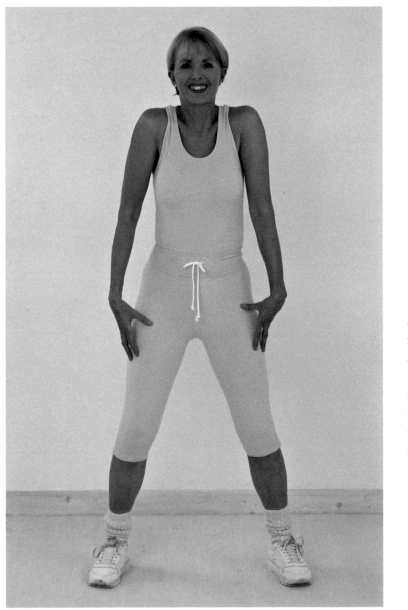

◁ **Ensure that you always warm up your muscles and adopt a good posture before starting any form of exercise. Stand with feet hip-width apart, knees slightly bent. Keep your spine straight and chin parallel to the floor. Lift your shoulders 5 times, hands resting on your thighs.**

Strengthening the arms

The following series of exercises are quick and easy to do anywhere and anytime of day. All you need is a couple of hand weights. Practised on a daily basis, you will soon notice the results.

△ **1** Arm lifts: stand with feet hip-width apart. Keep your knees soft and your spine straight. Taking a rice bottle in each hand, raise them above your head and circle your arms from the shoulder to increase flexibility and muscle tone. Repeat five times.

△ **2** Bicep curls: with a rice bottle in each hand, hold them down by your sides and then slowly bend your elbows to bring the bottles forward and upward until they reach your shoulders. Repeat five times.

△ **3** Triceps: lean forwards keeping your spine straight. You may find it easier to place one hand on the back of a chair to steady yourself. Holding a bottle by your side, slowly lift it behind you in a controlled movement. Do five times, then repeat with the other arm.

△ **4** Hold the bottles down by your sides, then slowly raise your arms out to the sides so that they are at 90 degrees to your body. Slowly lower your arms again. Repeat five times. This exercise helps prevent slack upper arms.

Flexibility exercise

Practising flexibility exercises on a regular basis helps to preserve the full range of motion in the joints, improves posture and helps to alleviate problems such as arthritis. Flexibility exercises are essentially stretching exercises. An excellent sequence of movements which will help to promote flexibility is found in "salute to the sun" – a yoga sequence that uses muscles throughout the body (see the section on yoga).

Strengthening the thighs

Practised regularly, the following exercise will strengthen the muscles in the outer thighs and increase flexibility in the hips.

▷ Lie on the floor on your side, body straight, with your head resting upon your lower arm for comfort and your upper arm resting beside your body. Now slowly raise your upper leg until it is as high as is comfortable, or use the seat of a dining chair as a guide. Hold the position for 5 seconds and repeat 5 times with each leg.

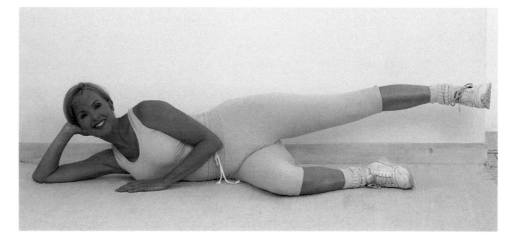

Choosing yoga

Yoga is one of the best ways to keep the joints and muscles flexible as you grow older. It can also relieve problems such as stress, anxiety, depression, back pain, asthma, hormonal imbalances, insomnia and irritable bowel syndrome. Although it has been practised in India for thousands of years, yoga did not appear in the West until the 19th century, and only became popular during the 1960s.

learning yoga

In the East, yoga is perceived as a route to spiritual enlightenment. In the West, however, the emphasis tends to be on yoga as a physical discipline. Western yoga classes usually focus on physical postures, known as asanas, and breathing techniques,

known as pranayama. The best way to learn yoga is from a trained teacher or therapist who will show you how to co-ordinate your breathing with your movement and help you to align your body correctly within the postures.

There are also plenty of books available to help you practise yoga at home. When practising alone, make sure that you do not push your body further than is comfortable and remember to start slowly and build your flexibility gradually; the people you see in yoga books have practised for years to become flexible.

Yoga teachers recommend practising for 30 to 60 minutes a day to gain full benefit, but many people find this difficult, and

20 minutes on a regular basis is sufficient to enhance energy and stamina levels, muscle tone, digestion, flexibility, strength and general wellbeing.

Salute to the sun

A sequence known as "salute to the sun" provides an excellent introduction to yoga. Traditionally, this is practised at sun rise, but you can practise it at any time of the day to achieve strength, flexibility and relaxation. Make your movements slow and rhythmic and pay attention to your breathing – the whole sequence should take between 10 and 15 minutes. Avoid this sequence of exercises if you are pregnant, injured or suffering from back pain.

◁ This basic yoga pose, the tree, is good for strengthening the pelvis, hip joints and shoulders.

Types of yoga

There are many different types of yoga. The type most widely practised in the West is "Hatha" ("ha" meaning "sun" and "tha" meaning "moon") representing the balancing and harmonization of positive and negative forces, usually through breathing and postures. Hatha yoga is just one branch of yoga and within Hatha yoga there are various "sub-categories":

- Astanga Vinyasa: a fast series of challenging postures performed using synchronized breathing. This is probably the most aerobic form of yoga.
- Iyengar: alignment and precision of movement are used to enhance posture, breathing and flexibility.
- Kundalini: breathing techniques and prana ("life force") are worked on to balance the body's energy and achieve relaxation.
- Sivananda: breathing and meditation are practised to produce a feeling of calm and inner peace.

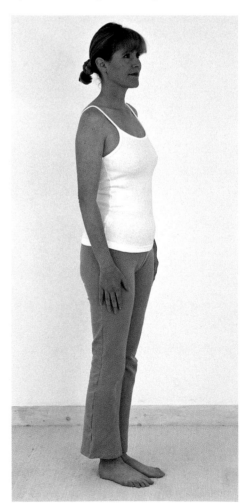

△ **1** Starting position

Stand upright with your hands at your sides, shoulders relaxed and your neck fully extended upwards.

△ **2** Look straight ahead and breathe out while bringing the palms of your hands together at chest height into the prayer position.

△ **3** Breathe in deeply and raise your hands slowly over your head until your thumbs meet. Raise your chest and arch your back as far as is comfortable.

△ **4** Exhale slowly and gently bend forward to touch the floor on either side of your feet (you may need to bend your knees). Bring your head in close to your knees.

△ **5** Breathing in deeply, extend your left leg behind you. Bend your right knee and bring it forward. Keep your hands flat on the floor as you extend your neck and look upward.

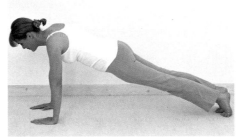

△ **6** Holding your breath, extend your right leg backwards to meet your left leg. Keep your hands flat on the floor. Take your weight on your hands and your toes. Keep your neck straight. Breathe out slowly and gradually lower your knees, chest and forehead to the floor.

△ **7** Keep your stomach and pelvic bones slightly raised. Breathing in deeply, lower your stomach and pelvis to the floor. Push up on your arms, and raise your chest. Extend your neck upwards. Bend your arms slowly and allow your chest to return to the floor.

△ **8** Next breathe out, raise your hips and pull yourself up into an arch. Your arms and legs should be fully extended – raise your hips as high as possible and lower your heels towards the floor.

△ **9-11** Breathing in deeply, repeat step 5, this time extending your right leg. Now breathe out slowly and bend forward as in step 4. Breathe in deeply as you raise your torso and repeat step 3.

△ **12** Breathe out slowly as you lower your arms and return to the starting position. Repeat the sequence.

The Pilates method

The Pilates method was devised by Joseph Pilates during the 1920s and has evolved over the years to offer both mental and physical training. It aims to increase body awareness, gently realign the body, enable efficient movement and enhance control of both body and mind.

The exercises

The best way to learn the Pilates method is in a class taught by an experienced teacher. The following exercises, however, can be practised at home. As with yoga, breathing is an important part of the Pilates method. **Try to breathe deeply into the lower ribcage during each exercise.**

△ **2** Relaxation position

Lie on your back with your knees bent, feet hip-width apart, head level so that your face is parallel to the floor, shoulders dropped and neck relaxed. Concentrate on your body as you allow yourself to sink into the floor.

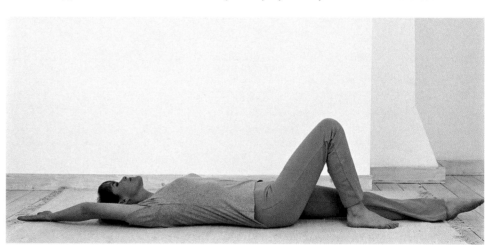

△ **3** Starfish

Lie on your back in the relaxation position. Breathe in and out deeply and slowly. As you breathe out, point your toes and slowly slide your left leg along the floor until it is fully stretched. Keep your right knee bent and your pelvis flat on the floor. At the same time, raise your right arm, as if swimming backstroke, until it rests along the floor above your head. Do not arch your spine. Breathe in and return to the start. Do this 6 times and then repeat with the right leg and left arm.

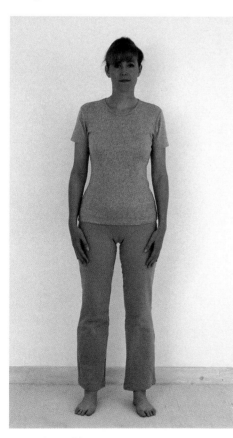

△ **1** Starting position

Stand up straight, drop the shoulders, lengthen and relax the neck, keep the feet parallel and hip-width apart and make sure the shoulders, spine and pelvis are all in line. Breathe in deeply and slowly so that you feel your lower ribcage expand. Keep your shoulders and neck relaxed. Breathe out at the same slow speed and repeat 6 times, concentrating as you do so.

▷ **4** Shoulder drops

Lie on your back in the relaxation position. Keeping both arms at shoulder height, raise your hands slowly towards the ceiling, palms facing each other. Leading with your fingertips, stretch one arm towards the ceiling so that your shoulder lifts off the floor. Now slowly drop the shoulder so that it rests flat against the floor again. Repeat 6 times with each arm and then return to the relaxation position.

▷ **5 The hundred**

Lie on your back in the relaxation position. Slowly bring your legs, one at a time, up towards your chest. Keep your arms flat by your sides, shoulders dropped and neck relaxed. Breathe in and out deeply and be aware of the stretch in your spine. Breathe in and raise your arms a little way off the floor and bring them down again. Repeat this, breathing in for the first five raises and breathing out for the next five raises. The aim is to reach a stage where you can raise and lower your arms 100 times, but you should start with ten raises and build up gradually.

The side-kick

This is an excellent exercise for strengthening the lower body. Have patience and work gradually through the exercise to achieve the best results. When practising the side-kick take care not to lift and lower your leg too quickly. It may help to visualize moving your leg through mud as this will slow you down. Your foot or knee should stay in line with your hip throughout the movement.

△ **1** Lie on your side, resting your head on your outstretched lower arm. Keep your head in line with your spine and your hips upright: they must not roll in or out. Bend your knees, one on top of the other. Place your free hand in front for balance but do not lean into the supporting arm or transfer your weight forward.

△ **2** Lift your top knee above your other knee and hold. Inhale and, with your toes pointed, move the top knee back behind your body as you exhale. The challenge is to keep your hips vertical and your abdominals hollowed. Your shoulder blades should be pulled down, your spine and your ribs should not be pushed up. You should feel this in your side.

△ **3** To make the exercise more challenging straighten both your legs. This should only be tried after practising the previous position first. Bring the bottom leg forward slightly from your hip, so it is not in line with your spine. Keep the hips vertical and lengthen out through both legs. Lift your top leg to hip height, inhale, and swing it to the front. Exhale as the leg travels backwards.

Controlled breathing

Learning to breathe correctly is an essential part of Pilates training. By breathing deeply into the lower ribcage and back out, you can ensure maximum use of your lung capacity. Try to breathe slowly, softly and rythmically to avoid any feeling of dizziness from overbreathing. The increase in oxygen supply provided by correct breathing will help the body replenish itself, while the exercise involved will help increase upper body flexibility. Never hold your breath during Pilates exercises as this will increase blood pressure, and waste energy in parts of the body where it is not needed.

Looking after the body

Many of the signs of aging are invisible because they occur inside the body and do not cause external changes. For example, over a period of many years, fatty deposits can build up on the walls of our arteries, leading to reduced blood flow and high blood pressure. We often only know this is happening when we experience symptoms. Fortunately, if we look after ourselves as we enter our 40s, 50s and 60s, by eating a healthy diet and getting plenty of exercise many age-related changes can be prevented.

The skeletal system

If you have healthy bones, the chances are that you will have an active and energetic later life. As you age, your mobility and range of movement depends largely on the health of your skeletal system. It is never too late to start looking after the health of your bones and by doing so you can help to prevent a range of problems including osteoporosis, arthritis and back pain.

osteoporosis

From your 30s onwards your bones gradually start to become thinner, less dense and more porous. This loss of bone density accelerates in women after the menopause and some go on to develop osteoporosis – a disease in which the bones are so weak that they fracture even on minor impact. Men can suffer from osteoporosis too, but it tends not to appear until much later in life.

People who have osteoporosis may have a hunched appearance resulting from compression of the vertebrae in the upper spine. They may also suffer from fractures of the wrist, hip or vertebrae. Risk factors for osteoporosis include family history, poor diet, lack of weight-bearing exercise, lack of sunlight, early menopause, smoking, high alcohol, coffee or salt intake, digestive problems, eating disorders, overuse of laxatives or commercial bran products and being underweight.

Incidences of osteoporosis are increasing dramatically in Europe and the USA. In the UK approximately 200,000 bone fractures occur as a direct result of osteoporosis each year, and of these cases 80,000 people die as a result, usually due to lung or blood complications caused by immobilization.

◁ **Light skipping can be a good exercise for muscle strength, lung capacity, circulation and joint strength, as well as weight control.**

preventing osteoporosis

The key to prevention is diet. The most important mineral for healthy bones is calcium and it is important not only to include enough calcium in the diet but also to make sure that calcium absorption and uptake into the bones is maximized.

Good sources of calcium in the diet are dairy products, almonds, brewer's yeast, parsley, globe artichokes, prunes, pumpkin seeds, cooked dried beans and cabbage. Try not to rely on high-fat dairy products such as milk and cheese to supply all your calcium needs. However, if you do drink milk, remember

that calcium is absorbed more efficiently in the presence of fat, so semi-skimmed milk is preferable to skimmed milk.

Factors that hinder calcium absorption include excess protein in the diet (over 40g/1$\frac{1}{2}$oz per day causes calcium to be excreted in the urine), excess caffeine

△ **Adding almonds to your diet is a tasty way to boost your intake of copper, magnesium, potassium, calcium, iron and zinc.**

△ **Sprinkle pumpkin seeds into dishes during cooking or on salads and cereals for added flavour and valuable nutrients such as zinc and iron.**

△ **Most of the vitamins and minerals in cabbage are contained in the dark outer leaves; but the inner leaves are still an excellent source of fibre.**

consumption and foods such as wheatbran, chocolate and rhubarb. Avoid these foods where possible.

Both cigarette smoking and drinking excessive amounts of alcohol can dramatically increase your risk of suffering from osteoporosis. As you grow older it is essential to quit smoking and restrict drinking to within government guidelines.

Since calcium is absorbed by the gut, it makes sense to look after your digestive system. Any form of bloating, flatulence or indigestion is a sign that the digestive system is not breaking down foods efficiently. If this is the case, consult a dietary therapist who may suggest taking digestive enzymes or going on an elimination diet to establish the cause of the problem.

If you know that you have a number of risk factors for osteoporosis, and you are a postmenopausal woman, ask your doctor about the possibility of having a bone density test and taking hormone replacement therapy (HRT). A course of HRT lasting a minimum of one year has been shown to improve bone density. You can also ask whether it is appropriate to take dietary supplements. There are some multivitamin and mineral

combinations that are specially formulated for postmenopausal women and a magnesium/calcium compound (in a 2:1 ratio) may also be of benefit. Other useful supplements may include 15mg doses of zinc citrate and 50mg doses of vitamin B complex.

Weight-bearing exercise, such as walking, has a key role to play in the prevention of osteoporosis. Try to go for a brisk 30-minute walk at least every other day.

The vinegar diet

Research at a Japanese University suggests that calcium absorption is facilitated in rats by giving them a diet rich in vinegar. Other research indicates that the amount of available calcium in chicken stock increases by 40 per cent when vinegar is added to the boiling liquid. It is thought that the acetic acid in vinegar breaks down the minerals in the bones in the stock. Dr Anthony Leeds of King's College, London suggests using vinegar as a condiment at meal times since it may enhance calcium uptake.

◁ **Large quantities of coffee are known to leach vitamins and minerals from the digestive system, increasing the risk of dietary malfunctions, and contributing to conditions such as osteoporosis.**

▷ **Nowadays vinegars come in a variety of flavours, making them an appetizing addition to many dishes.**

rheumatoid arthritis

Although doctors do not know the precise cause of rheumatoid arthritis it is thought to be an auto-immune disease in which the immune system starts to attack its own tissues. The most commonly affected areas are the hands and feet, followed by the knees, wrists, neck and ankles, although the disease can affect any joint in the body. Initial symptoms may include fatigue and fever followed by stiffness and swelling in the joints. Joint pain can become so bad that it restricts movement and in severe cases, bones may fuse together, making movement in the joint impossible.

Rheumatoid arthritis affects more women than men (in a 3:1 ratio) and usually appears between the ages of 40 and 50, although it can also appear in younger people, and is often accompanied by mild aneamia.

treating the symptoms of rheumatoid arthritis

You should always receive conventional medical diagnosis and treatment for rheumatoid arthritis. Doctors may recommend immuno-suppressant drugs or, in severe cases, joint replacement.

Complementary therapies can be useful for symptom relief. Dietary therapists may recommend limiting animal fats in the diet and taking supplements such as multivitamins, vitamin B complex, vitamin C, vitamin E (except when anti-coagulant drugs are being taken), glucosamine sulphate and zinc. An elimination diet may also be recommended if it is suspected that the disease is related to a food intolerance. Joint mobility can be helped by swimming, and pain can be eased by applying gentle heat to the area.

osteoarthritis

As the joints age they become prone to osteoarthritis. The cartilage in the joint wears away and the ends of the bones may rub together and develop growths which are known as spurs. The symptoms include joint pain that is exacerbated by movement, stiffness in the morning and bony growths on the fingers.

Osteoarthritis usually affects joints that have been subjected to excessive wear and tear. It is common in weight-bearing joints that have been overused in the past. Too much kneeling, for example, may cause osteoarthritis in the knees. There is no

△ This women's apalling posture is likely to lead to all sorts of health problems. When sitting you should always place both feet flat on the floor and ensure your back is straight in a chair which offers support to the small of the back.

definitive cure for osteoarthritis; treatment consists mainly of pain relief and, occasionally, joint replacement surgery. Being overweight places unnecessary stress on the joints, so an important part of preventative care is maintaining a healthy weight or losing weight if necessary. Try to keep joints as strong and as flexible as possible by taking regular exercise. A healthy diet that is low in saturated fats, and high in fish oils may also be helpful.

supportive action for osteoarthritis

It is thought that damaging substances known as free radicals may play a major part in arthritis. Taking an antioxidant supplement can help combat free radical damage to the joints. Dietary therapists also recommend taking a daily supplement of gamma-linolenic acid (GLA). If you suffer from osteoarthritis, you should avoid tasks,

◁ Since copper can be absorbed by the skin, many people find wearing a copper bracelet to be of use in the fight against bone disease.

◁ **Back problems are most commonly caused by lifting heavy objects incorrectly. Always bend at the knees and hips, taking the weight on your legs rather than your spine. Keep your back straight as you lift.**

preventing back complaints

The mainstay of preventative care is regular exercise that strengthens the back muscles. Both swimming and yoga are excellent. You should also pay careful attention to your posture when sitting, standing and lying. If you work at a desk make sure that it is at a comfortable height and that your chair offers lower back support. Be careful how you lift heavy items – always bend at the hips and knees, taking the weight on your legs and keeping your back straight. Never lift and twist at the same time.

△ **Lower back pain can be relieved by lying on your back, slowly lifting your knees and clasping them towards you. If you find this difficult, try lifting and clasping just one leg at a time and slowly build up to lifting both legs.**

such as carrying heavy bags, which place unnecessary stresses and strains on the affected joints. Swim regularly and consult a physiotherapist about specific exercises to prevent muscle wasting around the affected joints. Useful complementary treatments that you may wish to try include osteopathy and chiropractic.

back problems

As you grow older, everyday stresses and strains on the spine can build up and result in chronic back problems. The people most likely to suffer are manual workers, office workers, the overweight and the elderly. Back pain is usually caused by muscle or ligament strain or disc problems.

▷ **Camomile, eucalyptus, lavender and rosemary essential oils can be used in a warm bath or hot compress to help relieve back pain.**

Easing backache

If you have back pain, there are a number of things that you can do to relieve the pain.

• Lie flat on your back with your knees bent.

• Apply a cold compress to the affected area.

• Make a hot compress, of camomile, rosemary, eucalyptus and lavender essential oils. Allow up to 8 drops of essential oil per 100ml of hot water. Soak muslin in the water and oil, squeeze out excess and apply to the back. Place a warm towel over the compress and leave for at least 2 hours. (Eucalyptus may cause skin irritation, so use sparingly.)

• Hot showers may ease pain.

• Make sure your back is adequately supported by your chair and mattress.

• Sleep on your side with your knees bent and a pillow between them (or on your back with pillows beneath your knees).

The cardiovascular system

The chances of having a heart attack or a stroke increase with age and this is something that many people fear. You can help yourself by understanding the factors that put you at risk of problems and identifying those that are preventable. For example, although you cannot change your genetic predisposition, other risk factors such as poor diet, obesity and lack of exercise are within your control.

cardiovascular disease

As we grow older we become more prone to disease of the arterial walls. Over a period of years fatty deposits build up on the inner layers of the arteries and they gradually harden into plaques known as atheroma. As a result the arteries become narrow and the flow of blood is impeded. Another age-related change that affects the arteries is a gradual thickening and loss of elasticity of the walls. In combination, these changes are known as atherosclerosis.

Damage to the arteries around the heart caused by atherosclerosis can lead to conditions such as angina, in which the blood flow to the heart is restricted. The main symptom of angina is chest pain during exertion. If blood flow to the heart is blocked, the result is a heart attack. This can be fatal or it can cause long-term damage to the heart.

A stroke happens when the brain is deprived of oxygen as a result of a blockage in a blood vessel. This causes damage to the brain, which can be fatal or cause serious impairment. Hypertension refers to abnormally high blood pressure in the arteries caused by a hardening of the walls.

preventing cardiovascular disease

Since diet and lifestyle play such a major role in cardiovascular disease it is possible to make changes that drastically reduce your chances of becoming ill. The best preventative measures are:

• Eat a low-fat, high-fibre diet that includes plenty of oily fish, fruit and vegetables (see The anti-aging diet). This should become your permanent diet.
• If you are overweight, go on a weight-reduction diet. Consult your doctor about how much weight you need to lose and what types of food you should eat.
• Take aerobic exercise on a regular basis.

△ **Cook vegetables in a steamer to maintain the vitamins and minerals that are lost by boiling.**

Aerobic exercise gives your entire cardiovascular system a workout (see Staying fit throughout life). A brisk 30-minute walk taken at least three times a week can dramatically lower the risk of premature death.

• Cut down the amount of alcohol you drink to within established guidelines.
• Reduce the amount of stress in your life. Practise relaxation techniques, particularly meditation and yoga.
• Give up smoking.
• If you are a postmenopausal woman with a history of cardiovascular disease in your family, consult your doctor about taking hormone replacement therapy (HRT).
• If you suffer from diabetes, make sure that it is meticulously controlled. Consult your doctor about this.
• You should have regular health checks, particularly cholesterol tests and blood pressure checks.

◁ **A low-fat Mediterranean diet consisting of fish, fresh fruit and vegetables, olive oil and a small amount of red wine promotes good circulation.**

51

△ **Aerobic exercise taken three times a week strengthens the heart and increases blood flow.**

▽ **The shoulder rise stops blood from stagnating in the lower limbs of varicose vein sufferers.**

△ **Citrus fruit are rich in vitamin C.**

varicose veins

When the valves in the veins are weakened, preventing the proper flow of blood back towards the heart, varicose veins occur. Blood then stagnates in veins, usually in the lower limbs. Varicose veins appear as swollen, twisted clusters of purple or blue veins. They are more common in women than in men, and usually worsen with age, especially during pregnancy and the menopause.

fighting varicose veins

Preventative action against varicose veins includes taking regular exercise, eating a healthy and varied diet, weight control and avoiding long periods of standing. Complementary therapies that may be useful include aromatherapy, yoga, hydrotherapy, reflexology and naturopathy. A cold compress of witch hazel may be used to ease painful varicose veins.

Folic acid is another nutrient that is implicated in cardiovascular disease. It is thought to reduce the level of an amino acid, called homocysteine, which may cause arterial clogging and heart attacks. It is suggested that eating a bowl of cereal a day may be helpful. Apart from cereal, other good sources of folic acid include spinach, peanuts, broccoli, cauliflower, asparagus and sesame seeds.

Chocolate may have hidden health benefits. Research by scientists suggests that chocolate consumption can increase blood antioxidants. Drinking cocoa in moderation may have cardioprotective properties. However, most chocolate products are also high in fat and sugar.

▽ **Research in the US and Brazil has shown that moderate chocolate consumption increases blood antioxidants within two hours of ingestion.**

The digestive system

Some people find that the digestive system becomes sluggish and less efficient with age. If your diet has always been low in fibre and high in refined foods, digestive problems may make their first appearance in middle age. Some women first experience digestive disturbances around the time of the menopause.

digestive problems

Complaints that become more common with age are indigestion, bloating, constipation, flatulence and a condition known as diverticulosis. Diverticulosis occurs when pockets form in the intestinal wall. Food can become lodged in these pockets where it ferments, producing large amounts of gas. The sufferer typically experiences flatulence, bloating and abdominal discomfort. If the pockets become infected, this gives rise to a condition known as diverticulitis. The symptoms of this are abdominal cramping, nausea and fever.

Apart from poor dietary habits, one reason why older people may suffer from digestive problems is that hydrochloric acid production declines with age. Hydrochloric acid is released from the stomach wall and it begins the breakdown of protein in the stomach. If you notice that you are prone to indigestion after eating high-protein foods, you may not be producing enough stomach acid. One solution to this is to take a digestive supplement containing betaine hydrochloride.

preventing digestive problems

The best way to prevent digestive problems is to eat a high-fibre diet. Fibre is not digested by the body so it passes through the gut intact, effectively "exercising" the intestines and adding bulk to stools. It is important to remember that if you increase the amount of fibre in your diet you should also increase the

△ **Baked potatoes are a good, low-fat source of dietary fibre when eaten with the skin.**

amount of water that you drink. This is because fibre swells and absorbs water in the intestines.

Foods that are rich in fibre include oats, baked potatoes, lentils, brown rice, beans, fruit, wholegrain bread and wholewheat cereals. Eating cruciferous vegetables, such as broccoli and cabbage, several times a week may help to reduce the risk of colon cancer. Getting plenty of exercise is another important way of ensuring digestive health.

supportive action for digestive problems

One way of testing how well your digestive system is working is by timing how long it takes for food to pass through your system. This is known as "transit time".

To do the transit test, include a test food in your diet that you would not normally eat. It should be a food, such as beetroot, that will be visible in your stools. Alternatively, you can use charcoal tablets from a pharmacy. The time between eating the food and its first appearance in your stools should be 12–14 hours. The colour should disappear from your stools after

△ **Commercial bran and laxatives should be avoided where possible. Instead eat oats, which hold water and stimulate bowel movements.**

36–48 hours (this is called the retention time). If the transit time is significantly longer than 14 hours and retention time is 72 hours or more, then this is a sign that your bowel function is sluggish.

Sluggish bowel function can be treated by a wide range of complementary therapies such as massage, acupuncture, acupressure, homeopathy, herbalism and naturopathy. Naturopaths may recommend going on a cleansing diet that gives your gut a chance to clear itself. The best self-help treatment is gradually including more fibre in your diet. You should avoid taking commercial laxatives and bran products, which do not allow the body to assimilate nutrients fully, and can be harsh on the body. Specific problems may be alleviated by a number of herbal or dietary remedies.

△ **Fennel can be useful in controlling flatulence.**

△ **Liquorice can help keep bowel movements regular.**

△ **Eating ginger is an excellent remedy for nausea.**

△ **Garlic and onion are good for cleansing the digestive system.**

- Garlic, peppermint, camomile and fennel may relieve flatulence.
- Linseed, prunes, rhubarb, ginger, chilli, liquorice, olive oil and honey may help to relieve mild constipation.
- Tea made with ginger root may help to alleviate nausea.
- Garlic and onions may help to cleanse the digestive system.
- Psyllium husks may help to relieve constipation. They are available in capsule form from health food shops.

▷ **Advances in dental care mean that dentures will soon be a thing of the past.**

Colon cleansing formulas are also available.
- Broad spectrum digestive enzymes, which can be bought from health food shops, may be helpful in the treatment of indigestion.
- A supplement containing acidophilus and bifidus bacteria can ensure a healthy bacterial environment in the gut.

Early warning signs

If you have any unusual or persistent digestive symptoms, such as a sudden, inexplicable change in bowel movements, blood in the stools or pain in the abdomen, consult your doctor.

Maintaining healthy teeth

The process of digestion begins in the mouth when we chew our food. Chewing has a valuable function: it increases the surface area of the food so that it is easier for enzymes to break down nutrients into their basic components. If your teeth are in poor health, they cannot perform their function properly and you will be restricted in the types of food you can eat. Pay meticulous attention to dental hygiene as you get older, visit a dentist regularly and use disclosing tablets and floss after brushing to identify and remove plaque. Gum recession, which can cause teeth to become loose in their sockets, is one of the main problems that arises with age. Try not to encourage this process: use a soft toothbrush and avoid brushing the gums.

Looking after your eyesight

The senses often become blunted with age. Changes tend to take place very gradually. If you experience a sudden change in your ability to see or hear, consult a doctor as it may be a sign of underlying illness.

vision problems

The eyes undergo a number of changes as you grow older. The lens becomes more opaque and loses its flexibility, the iris becomes sluggish, the retina can become less sensitive to light, and a condition called glaucoma – in which pressure builds up inside the eye – becomes more likely. On average, the eye of a 60-year-old person lets in half as much light as a younger person's. The most common type of age-related vision change is long-sightedness.

Warning signs of eye problems are as follows:
• difficulty seeing objects close-up (this may be caused by long sightedness)
• hazy vision, a blur around lights and the sensation of looking through fog (this may be caused by cataracts)
• loss of peripheral vision, flashes of light and floating shapes (this may be caused by retinal detachment)

△ You should always ensure that your sunglass lenses are scratch free, otherwise they may do more harm to your eyesight than good.

• rapid or gradual vision loss and distorted vision when reading (this may be caused by macular degeneration)
• blurred vision, sudden and severe eye pain, teary, aching eyes, halos around lights, headache, nausea and vomiting (this may be caused by glaucoma).

You should have your eyesight tested yearly as you get older, and consult your doctor or ophthalmologist about any

◁ Glaucoma may occur in people over the age of 40. Nutritionists suggest a diet rich in vitamin A may be of assistance in protecting sight.

The Bates method

This is a series of eye exercises that may help to improve vision.

- splash the eyes with warm water 10 times and then cold water 10 times to increase blood circulation to the eyes.
- twice a day, rest your elbows on a table and cup your hands over your eyes. Allow yourself to relax for 10 minutes. If you do a lot of close up or computer work try to do this for one minute on a regular basis.
- try not to stare rigidly at any object for a long period of time. Every five minutes look away briefly and focus on something else for a few seconds.
- to strengthen the eye muscles, hold one index finger 10cm/4in in front of your eyes, and place the other index finger at arm's length behind it. Focus with both eyes on the nearest finger for a few seconds, blink, and then focus on the distant finger. Repeat this exercise 10 times, blinking between each change of focus to lubricate and clean the eyes.

▷ **By splashing the eyes with warm and then cold water, circulation can be increased which may help against sight degeneration.**

changes in your vision. The treatment for eye problems ranges from reading glasses for long-sightedness to surgery for cataracts. If you have adult-onset diabetes, you should be particularly vigilant about having regular eye checks – diabetes is one of the main causes of blindness.

Try to protect your eyes as much as possible by not working in poor light, avoiding spending hours in front of a computer, learning some basic Bates method exercises, eating a healthy diet and taking regular exercise to increase the blood supply to the eyes. You should also wear sunglasses in bright light.

▽ **Always remove contact lenses or glasses before practising any eye exercises.**

Smell, taste and hearing

hearing problems

Problems with hearing may occur as we age due to deterioration of the sensory nerve cells and the minuscule hairs within the inner ear. Loss of hearing is a very gradual process that actually starts at the beginning of life: from the moment we are born the tiny hairs in the inner ear start to die. All of us, as we age, lose the ability to hear high-pitched sounds as clearly as when we were young. Rumbling base sounds, on the other hand, become clearer.

Age-related hearing loss is known as presbycusis. It is common in men over 40 and may be genetically influenced. Because it can be accelerated by exposure to loud noise, it is very important to avoid exposure to repetitive noise, such as music or drilling. Hearing loss is gradual and you should look out for the following warning signs:
• difficulty hearing high frequencies
• difficulty understanding speech
• difficulty hearing in noisy places
• being unable to hear sounds you used to
Consult your doctor at the first sign of hearing loss. The main treatment for age-related deafness is a hearing aid. Some people benefit from learning lip reading and sign language. Complementary treatments that may help to improve hearing include reflexology and osteopathy.

Tinnitus is another age-related problem. It presents itself as a continuous high-pitched ringing, buzzing, humming, hissing or whistling that only the sufferer can hear. There are various causes including prolonged exposure to loud noise, high blood pressure, blockage with wax, ear infection and a perforated eardrum. Some drugs cause tinnitus as a side-effect.

The best way to prevent tinnitus is to wear ear plugs in noisy situations. You should also get plenty of rest, minimize stress and limit your salt intake. Playing soft music,

▷ **Consult your doctor if you begin to have difficulty following conversations.**

▷Your sense of smell may be heightened by eating zinc-rich foods such as peanuts or ginger root.

exercising regularly, practising relaxation techniques and avoiding smoking and alcohol may ease symptoms.

smell

Our sense of smell is a much neglected asset. As well as protecting us in dangerous situations – alerting us to a fire, for example – it can also influence mood. Aromatherapists rely heavily on the olfactory system for their work. Receptors in the nose absorb smells that stimulate the olfactory bulb. Signals are then transmitted to the limbic system – part of the brain involved in the control of emotions. As you age your sense of smell is blunted and it becomes harder to differentiate between smells. Combined with a loss of taste this can mean that food becomes less appetizing

taste

There are an average of 10,000 taste buds on the tongue, the roof of the mouth, the pharynx and the oesophagus. When you are young these taste buds are replaced on a regular basis but, with age, the replacement process becomes less efficient. This means that food may not taste as interesting or diverse as it used to as you get older. Smoking, drinking alcohol and certain medications can exacerbate this. People who wear dentures may suffer additionally because the taste receptors in the palate are covered. Women may not notice any decline in their ability to taste until after menopause when oestrogen levels decline.

Although a decline in sense of taste and smell may not seem to present a serious problem, it can mean that older people start to compensate by eating different foods. For example, they may start to avoid fruit and vegetables because they taste bland, and concentrate instead on salty food, sauces and strongly flavoured cheese and meat. This can have serious implications for health. A diet with a high salt content is associated with high blood pressure, and a diet rich in saturated fat is linked to cardiovascular disease. Dietary therapists say that a decline in taste and smell may be due to a lack of zinc and that, when

zinc-rich foods are eaten in the diet, taste and smell become more acute. Examples of zinc-rich food are oysters, ginger root, pecan nuts, brazil nuts, peanuts, wholewheat grains, dry split peas and egg yolk. If you want to add flavour to foods, try to use herbs and spices rather than salt.

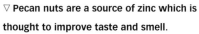
▽ Pecan nuts are a source of zinc which is thought to improve taste and smell.

△ To avoid overuse of salt, try adding herbs and spices to enhance flavour.

Overcoming stress

Research shows that your stress levels can have a profound effect on your health. If you suffer from chronic stress you may exist in a permanent state of physiological arousal: your heart beat and blood pressure are constantly elevated and stress hormones such as adrenaline are circulating in your bloodstream. Chronic stress is implicated in a number of age-related health problems, the main one being cardiovascular disease.

what is stress?

Stress is a physiological survival mechanism. When you sense that you are under threat, the brain responds by sending a message to the adrenal glands on top of your kidneys, which, in turn, respond by releasing adrenaline. Adrenaline has effects on various body systems that, in combination, enable you to take action: to either run away from the source of the threat or to stay and fight it. This is known as the "fight or flight response".

Although this physiological response may have been useful in primitive times, when humans needed to literally fight or run away from sources of danger, it is less useful in modern society, where sources of threat are mainly psychological. For example, a contemporary source of stress

might be travelling to work on crowded public transport when you are already late for a meeting. Your brain registers stress but you will not be able to take advantage of the subsequent adrenaline rush because no physical action is necessary.

When instances of stress are occasional and short-lived, the body can cope (some degree of stress helps us to stay motivated and to meet our goals), but when they are frequent and long-lasting the body may be perpetually in a state of high alert. This is when your vulnerability to problems such as cardiovascular disease increases. For this reason, it is essential to find ways to overcome chronic stress as you get older.

dietary support

People often turn to "quick fixes" when they are under stress. They feel tired, irritable and lacking in energy and they often turn to chocolate, caffeine or alcohol for stress relief, or a quick energy burst. Unfortunately, these substances deplete the body of energy and make you feel worse.

The most important nutrients to include in the diet when you are under stress are the B vitamins, vitamin C, zinc, chromium and magnesium. Dietary therapists may recommend taking a multivitamin and

△ **Eating bananas rather than refined-sugar products can boost natural sugar levels, which helps to combat stress.**

mineral supplement that supplies these nutrients. It is also very important to avoid sugary foods when under stress because they stimulate the stress hormone cortisol. Instead, eat foods such as bananas, wholegrains, seeds, beans and lentils.

yoga, meditation and breathing

Learning relaxation techniques is a powerful antidote to stress. Yoga and meditation teach you how to still the mind

◁ **Breathing techniques can be a useful way to reduce stress at work.**

▷ **Relaxation techniques can help in the fight against stress-induced digestive disorders such as ulcers and indigestion.**

and focus on something simple such as the breath flowing in and out of your body. When you are stressed your breathing is usually fast and shallow. Making a conscious effort to relax your muscles and breathe deeply can help you to overcome stress. Yoga and meditation techniques are best learned from a trained therapist or teacher, but there are also plenty of books available.

One useful meditation technique is the humming bee practice. Sit in a comfortable position and close your eyes. Focus on the breath entering and leaving your nostrils. Say to yourself: "I am aware of breathing in. I am aware of breathing out". Use your fingers to close your ear flaps and imagine the sound of a humming bee inside your head. Breathe in and, as you breathe out, make the sound of a humming bee. Breathe in and repeat. Try to concentrate on the sound and on your breathing. Regular practice of this exercise should help to still your mind.

aromatherapy and massage

A range of complementary therapies can help to ease stress: acupuncture, reflexology, hypnotherapy, homeopathy and flower remedies. Aromatherapy and massage are very widely used in the treatment of stress and aromatherapists recommend the following essential oils: basil, bergamot, clary sage, camomile, geranium, hyssop, juniper, lavender, marjoram, thyme, cedar, neroli, rose and sandalwood. Massage can help to ease stress by relieving muscle tension and enhancing circulation.

Try a stress-relieving bath consisting of 2 drops each of camomile and marjoram, and 4 drops of juniper. Alternatively, try a drop each of camomile, juniper and marjoram dropped onto a tea bag and put in a large cup of hot water during times of stress.

personal stress-beaters

Everyone has their own ways of overcoming stress and it is important to cultivate methods that work for you. Some people unwind by talking to friends or a partner or by being sociable, others relax by spending time on their own. Exercise is a stress-beating technique that works for many people as it uses up adrenaline. The

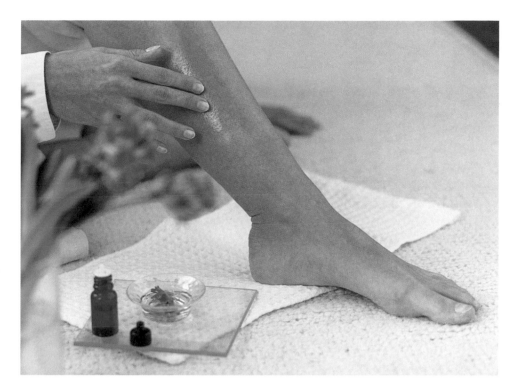

△ **Taking time to massage yourself with stress-relieving essential oils can be a good antidote to stress.**

▷ **Herbal teas and Bach Flower Remedies are quick and effective cures for stress.**

endorphin rush that exercise brings can also provide a sense of well-being.

Sometimes a change of attitude can turn a stressful situation into a non-stressful one: ask yourself if a situation can be turned to your advantage in any way. Some people decide that, rather than trying to relieve the symptoms of stress, they will tackle the underlying cause. This may involve leaving a stressful job or ridding yourself of other responsibilities you can no longer manage.

Pet ownership can have a remarkable effect on stress levels. Pets act as morale boosters by offering unconditional loyalty. They can provide a valuable outlet for people who find it difficult to express their emotions – this in itself is cathartic.

▷ **By allowing us to care for them, pets can make us feel needed and appreciated.**

understanding depression

Many psychologists make a distinction between depressed mood and depression. Depressed mood describes the temporary sensation of "feeling down" that you have when something goes wrong in your life. Depression, on the other hand, is more intense and long-lasting. It can affect your behaviour, your relationships, your eating and sleeping patterns and your entire world view. The likelihood of depression may increase as you grow older. Elderly people, in particular, are more prone to suffering from depression.

recognizing the signs

Feelings of dejection, hopelessness and inadequacy are the most common signs of depression. But depression can manifest itself in a variety of ways and it is important to be aware of the signs, both in yourself and in others.

• Loss of interest in everyday activities
• Excessive sleeping or insomnia
• Fatigue and lack of energy
• Feelings of hopelessness and worthlessness
• Loss of sexual interest
• Apathy
• Excessive overeating or undereating
• Dejection, sadness and crying
• Problems with concentration and remembering things
• Difficulty making decisions
• Indifference to the world around you
• Suicidal thoughts and urges

what causes depression?

Depression can be triggered by a specific event. Life events that are associated with depression include divorce, separation, bereavement (particularly of a close family member), or being fired or made redundant. Sometimes depression has no specific or obvious cause. Depression that occurs in older people may result from a perceived loss of control in life. The prospect of growing older may in itself be depressing,

△ **Getting at least 15 minutes of bright sunlight and fresh air every day, preferably by taking a brisk walk in full daylight, can help to banish feelings of depression.**

especially given the fact that many societies tend to devalue aging and equate power and sexuality with youthfulness.

self-help for depression

If you feel depressed, try to make sure that you continue to eat and sleep properly. Avoid resorting to destructive props such as alcohol, cigarettes or drugs. Make sure that your diet is high in vitamin C, B vitamins, essential fatty acids and unrefined carbohydrates. Avoid refined, sugary foods.

If possible, stay active, exercise regularly (the endorphins released during exercise can help to combat depression) and seek the support of friends and family. Speak about how you are feeling and do not be afraid to express negative emotions such as fear, guilt, anger or sadness. Complementary therapies may help to combat depression. Herbalists

▷ **Taking time out to practise meditation may help you to relax and forget your worries.**

△ A sluggish digestive system can cause and increase feelings of depression, so ensure a high fibre intake is maintained.

◁ Vitamin C is essential in the fight against depression, yet it is depleted by stress.

recommend taking St. John's wort for depression, although long-term use of the herb may cause sensitivity to light. Aromatherapists say that essential oils such as basil, bergamot, clary sage, camomile, geranium, lavender, thyme, jasmine, neroli (orange blossom), rose, sandalwood and ylang ylang can help to lift mood, especially if used in combination with massage.

Understanding some of the cognitive processes that underpin depression can be helpful. The cognitive psychologist, Aaron Beck, says that depressed people often make "errors" in their thinking. If possible, try to challenge the following thought processes when they happen to you:

- Overgeneralization: the depressed person makes sweeping, negative generalizations. For example, "my whole life is pointless".
- Selective abstraction: the depressed person focuses on small negative details. For example, from a list of compliments, the depressed person remembers a chance remark that could be construed as negative.
- Magnification and minimization: the depressed person dramatizes the importance of negative events and downplays the importance of positive events. For example, a man who is not invited to a party sees himself as a social failure despite the fact that he has recently had an enjoyable meeting with some old friends.

- Personalization: the depressed person takes responsibility for things beyond his control. For example, "Today's train strike has happened because I need to get somewhere urgently".
- Arbitrary inference: the depressed person infers something without justification. For example, a woman infers from her husband's angry expression that she has done something wrong. If she had enquired further she would have discovered that her husband was angry about something unrelated to her.

△ Time spent making your surroundings more enjoyable can enhance your appreciation of life.

△ A warm, relaxing bath using uplifting aromatherapy oils can help against depression.

seeking professional help for depression

If you are suffering from depression you should consult your doctor. Treatment for depression consists of anti-depressant medication or psychotherapy, sometimes a combination of the two. There are different types of psychotherapy ranging from counselling to cognitive therapy to psychoanalysis. Discuss with your doctor which type meets your needs. If you are taking any complementary medicine, inform your doctor.

Thinking positively

Optimism, enthusiasm and a refusal to tolerate boredom are characteristics that are often associated with young people. There is no reason why this should be the case, however, and one of the best ways to remain psychologically young is to cultivate the art of positive thinking.

foster a sense of optimism

Life brings many experiences: some positive and some negative. As people get older they may fall into the trap of focusing on negative experiences and unwittingly cultivating a sense of pessimism about the future.

and physical health – it can even boost your immunity to illness. Make a list of the life experiences that have affected you positively and negatively. Compare the positive list with the negative list. Ask yourself if anything from the negative list can be discarded or turned into a positive situation. Congratulate yourself on your achievements in life and concentrate on the future rather than the past.

Optimism is cultivated by keeping busy and active. Take up activities that make you feel good about yourself such as yoga, walking or swimming. Learn something

distance yourself from problems

If there are situations and problems in your life that you find inescapable, try to distance yourself from them. Take an overview: tell yourself that this is one episode in your life and it will not last indefinitely. If possible, try to see humour in difficult situations. Imagine that you are a stranger walking past the window of your own house. What would the stranger see? What would the stranger make of the events going on?

Ask yourself whether your current problems will still affect you in a year's time

◁ By making a list of positive and negative aspects of our lives, we enable ourselves to see the areas needing attention.

▷ Planning a holiday can cheer you up by giving you something to look forward to.

Pessimism can be further encouraged by media messages that value youth and denigrate aging.

Resolve to clear out your emotional baggage and foster a sense of optimism about the present and the future. Optimism has huge benefits for both psychological

completely new. Make sure that you are always working towards new goals and challenges. Set up a timetable in which to meet these goals. For example: "by the end of the year I will have converted one room of the house into a studio for painting, reading and music practice".

or in five or ten years? If you can, let go of things that you cannot change and concentrate on the things that you can. Remember that, even if you cannot change a situation, you always have the option of changing the way that you think about it. Cultivate a sense of control.

Lock up your problems

When you are confronted with a negative situation or a problem, try the following visualization technique. Imagine that you have a small wooden box with a lock and key. Visualize the people or situations that are upsetting you and then open the box and carefully place them inside. Lock the box and put the key in your pocket. Place the box in a dark drawer and tell yourself that it stays there until you are ready to take it out and unlock it. When you are ready to deal with it, then do so. In the meantime, if the problem becomes greater, visualize taking the box out of the drawer, giving it a shake, and then replacing it.

have a mental clear-out

One negative stereotype of aging is that our beliefs become more rigid and inflexible as we get older. Challenge this assumption by discarding old beliefs and values. A belief that you have held for years may no longer be useful to you, it may be outdated or experience may have taught you new lessons. Question your beliefs about everything from gender roles to politics. Also question your beliefs about yourself. If you find yourself thinking you are incapable of doing something, ask yourself why.

Have a physical clear out as well as a mental and emotional one. If you make the symbolic gesture of throwing out clothes and other possessions that you have not used for years, this will reinforce your feelings of positivity and change.

enjoy the simple things

Think positively about small things in life as well as big things. Derive pleasure from everyday activities such as cooking meals, bathing and reading a book or newspaper. Immerse yourself in whatever you are doing. Take the time to look at your surroundings. If you always travel by public transport, try making the effort to walk once in a while.

Friendships are important in helping us to think positively. Friends provide support, companionship, humour and affection, as well as a valuable buffer against stress.

▷ Dogs have an unlimited capacity for enjoyment which can be infectious.

▽ Taking time to enjoy the company of a good friend can change a dull day into a good one.

The importance of sleep

Sleep is essential to your mental and physical well being. If you do not have sufficient sleep, you are likely to become moody and bad-tempered. If your insomnia is chronic, you may be permanently tired, lacking in energy and depressed. Although sleeping patterns change as you grow older, getting a good night's sleep remains essential for the regular rejuvenation of the body.

why do we need sleep?

Sleep experts are not sure about the precise functions of sleep but it is thought that the body needs a period of rest every night to allow it to recuperate from the day and to repair cellular damage and maintain the immune system. Cells all over the body have the chance to regenerate and the brain consolidates what has happened during the day into long-term memory. People who are deprived of sleep may suffer from mood swings, irritability and psychoses.

sleep and aging

There is a popular misconception that people need less sleep as they grow older. In fact, your sleep requirements remain fairly constant throughout adulthood. Most people need approximately eight hours a night whether they are young or old. However, a variety of changes take place in sleeping patterns as people grow older and these changes conspire to make the overall duration of sleep shorter than before.

Sleep experts say that the "architecture" of sleep changes with age. Older people spend less time in deep sleep or "delta sleep" than younger people. Although they continue to spend the same amount of time in dream or "rapid eye movement" (REM) sleep as younger people.

People may find it more difficult to get to sleep as they grow older and this may be because they produce less of the chemicals that control the sleep/waking cycle. For

△ **If menopausal hot flushes keep you awake during the night, keep a fan, sponge and water beside your bed, so that you can easily cool yourself down.**

example, older people secrete less melatonin, a sleep-promoting substance produced by the pineal gland in the brain.

Other age-related changes to sleeping patterns include waking up more frequently and spending more time awake during the night. Generally, people adapt to these natural changes and do not find them debilitating.

problems with sleep

There are a number of specific problems that affect people's sleep as they grow older. For example, menopausal women may find their sleep is disrupted by hot flushes or night sweats. Typically, women wake up at intervals throughout the night feeling hot, feverish and drenched in sweat. They may need to change their bed clothes and bed linen, which adds to sleep disruption. In the long term this can lead to poor concentration, irritability, depression and reduced immune system efficiency. If your sleep is severely disrupted by night sweats, you should consult your doctor.

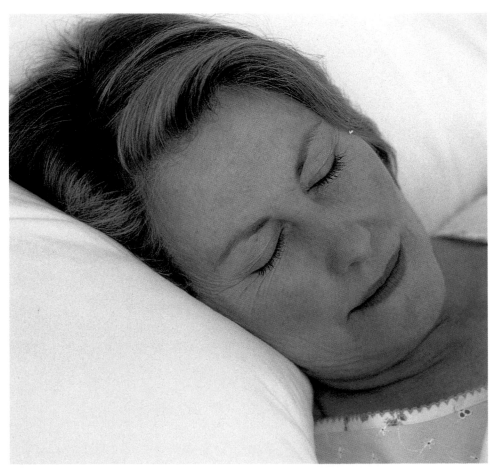

◁ **Skin cells regenerate at a much faster rate during sleep, so a good night's rest is important to a healthy body.**

△ Making your bedroom welcoming and relaxing can help to induce sleep.

Immediate self-help measures include keeping a bowl of water, a sponge, a hand-held fan and a towel by your bedside. Always wear night clothes made of natural fibres and keep a change of night clothes beside the bed.

Some age-related illnesses may interfere with sleep patterns. The aches and pains associated with arthritis can make it difficult to get to sleep and can disrupt sleep throughout the night. Digestive problems such as gastro-oesophageal reflux can abbreviate sleep. This is a disorder where

Daytime napping

Opinions are mixed about the value of napping during the day. If you are suffering from insomnia, it can exacerbate it. Also, rather than compensating for insomnia, you should try to discover and treat the underlying cause. On the other hand, by training our bodies to accept short periods of sleep when we need it we can avoid overstretching our systems during the day.

there is a backflow of stomach acid into the oesophagus. Sufferers may find that sleep problems can be resolved simply by raising their heads up off the bed.

Other age-related illnesses that can interfere with sleep patterns include cancer, osteoporosis, Parkinson's disease, bladder problems and cardiovascular disease. Some prescribed medications may also be responsible for disrupting your sleep. Diuretic drugs may cause you to get up frequently during the night to visit the bathroom.

Insomnia can sometimes have a psychological origin. If you are depressed, upset or anxious, for example, then sleep is

likely to be elusive. You should consult your doctor if you frequently suffer from chronic insomnia – it is important that the underlying cause is diagnosed and treated correctly.

On the other hand, a daytime nap can be a valuable way to relieve fatigue and sleepiness. If your night sleep is temporarily being disrupted and you are not usually an insomnia sufferer, a short nap during the day (before 3:00 pm if possible) can revive and refresh you, and give you the energy to keep going through the remainder of the day.

▽ Try to take cat naps before 3:00 pm to avoid disturbing your ability to fall asleep at nightime.

Quality sleep

coping with snoring

Snoring increases with age. It is not usually a sign of a serious problem, although it can disrupt the sleep of a partner. Snoring results when the airways are obstructed, usually because the muscles that keep them open are too lax or because there is a build up of fatty tissue around the airways. Anything that encourages muscle relaxation, from lying on your back to drinking alcohol, may make snoring worse. The noise of snoring comes from the air rattling over the relaxed tissues of the palate and throat.

Snoring is most common in middle-aged people who are overweight. There are several preventative measures:

• Lose weight.
• Avoid drinking alcohol or eating heavily before you go to bed.
• Sleep without a pillow.
• Quit smoking. Smoking is a major cause of airway congestion.
• Sleep on your side rather than on your back. You can force yourself to do this by sewing a tennis ball into the back of your nightclothes.

sleep apnea

Occasionally, snoring may be associated with a serious disorder known as sleep apnea which becomes more common in middle and later life. Sleep apnea occurs when the upper airway becomes blocked and prevents you from breathing. In severe cases, sleep apnea may result in high blood pressure and increase your risk of heart attack and stroke.

During the night the apnea sufferer stops breathing, levels of oxygen in the bloodstream fall rapidly and the sufferer wakes up briefly, gasps for breath and then falls asleep again. This happens over and over again throughout the night and often means that the sufferer feels extremely sleepy during the day. Sleep apnea may be accompanied by loud snoring and is most common in overweight or obese people. If sleep apnea is mild, it may be overcome by

△ Practising relaxation exercises before going to bed may help you to overcome insomnia.

◁ A lavender sachet beside the bed, or a few drops of lavender oil on your pillow may enduce sleep.

weight loss, lying on your side and avoiding smoking, alcohol and sedative medications. If it is severe, a doctor may recommend keeping the airways open with a special device or, sometimes, with surgery.

learning to relax

One of the best ways of enhancing sleep is learning an effective method of relaxation. Complementary therapies, such as aromatherapy, massage, acupuncture and flower remedies, can help you to relax and overcome insomnia. T'ai chi and yoga are also very useful. Or you can try the following creative visualization exercise.

Lie flat on your back with your arms by your sides, palms up, and your legs straight and hip-width apart. Breathe in and out deeply. Try to draw the breath down into your abdomen so that your lungs are taking in the maximum amount of oxygen to replenish your body. Close your eyes and focus your thoughts on a single item that

▷ **A warm aromatherapy bath before bedtime can relax muscles and emotions.**

▽ **Leave an aromatherapy burner alight whilst you prepare for bed to help your body and mind relax.**

you find relaxing, such as a cloud, a tree, a lake or the sea. Concentrate on the qualities – the texture, depth, colour and movement – of the image you have chosen. If any distracting thoughts come into your head, acknowledge them and then visualize them as leaves being gently blown away. Keep breathing deeply into your abdomen. When you are ready to finish your relaxation session, do so slowly. Let your thoughts return to the room you are in and gently move your toes and fingers. Roll onto one side and get up. Alternatively, you can do this exercise in bed before you go to sleep.

Enhancing sleep quality

Try to maximize your sleep quality by making your environment as comfortable as possible and by developing good sleeping habits.

- Make sure your bedroom is relaxing, warm and well aired.
- Burn lavender essential oil in an aromatherapy burner in your bedroom. Or put a handkerchief with a few drops of lavender oil under your pillow.
- Avoid eating a heavy meal immediately before going to bed.

△ **Some foods, such as turkey, avocado, cottage cheese, milk and bananas contain tryptophan which may assist healthy sleep.**

- Avoid caffeinated drinks or alcohol before you go to bed. Although alcohol can speed up the onset of sleep, it disrupts the pattern of sleep at a later stage in the night.
- Go to bed at roughly the same time every night (preferably later rather than earlier).
- Get up at roughly the same time every morning, even if you go to bed later than usual.
- If possible, use your bedroom for sleep only (rather than for work, watching television or talking on the telephone, for example). This way your brain will learn to associate the bedroom with sleep.
- Make sure your bed is comfortable and supports your spine. If you have a back problem, try sleeping on your side with your knees bent and a pillow between them.
- Cut out any sources of light that may keep you awake.
- Eliminate irritating noises. Fix dripping taps and noisy plumbing or radiators. Alternatively, buy some good quality ear plugs.
- Wear night clothes made from natural fibres.
- Have a warm bath and a milky drink before going to bed. Try the following essential oils in your bath: 2 drops each of camomile and rose with 4 drops each of juniper and marjoram, or 2 drops each of camomile and juniper and 4 drops of neroli.

△ **Listening to relaxing music before bedtime helps many people to switch from an active to a passive state of mind.**

- Eating foods that contain the amino acid tryptophan may help you to sleep. These include avocado, turkey, cottage cheese, milk and bananas.
- Do something relaxing and enjoyable, such as reading a book or listening to soothing music, before you go to bed.

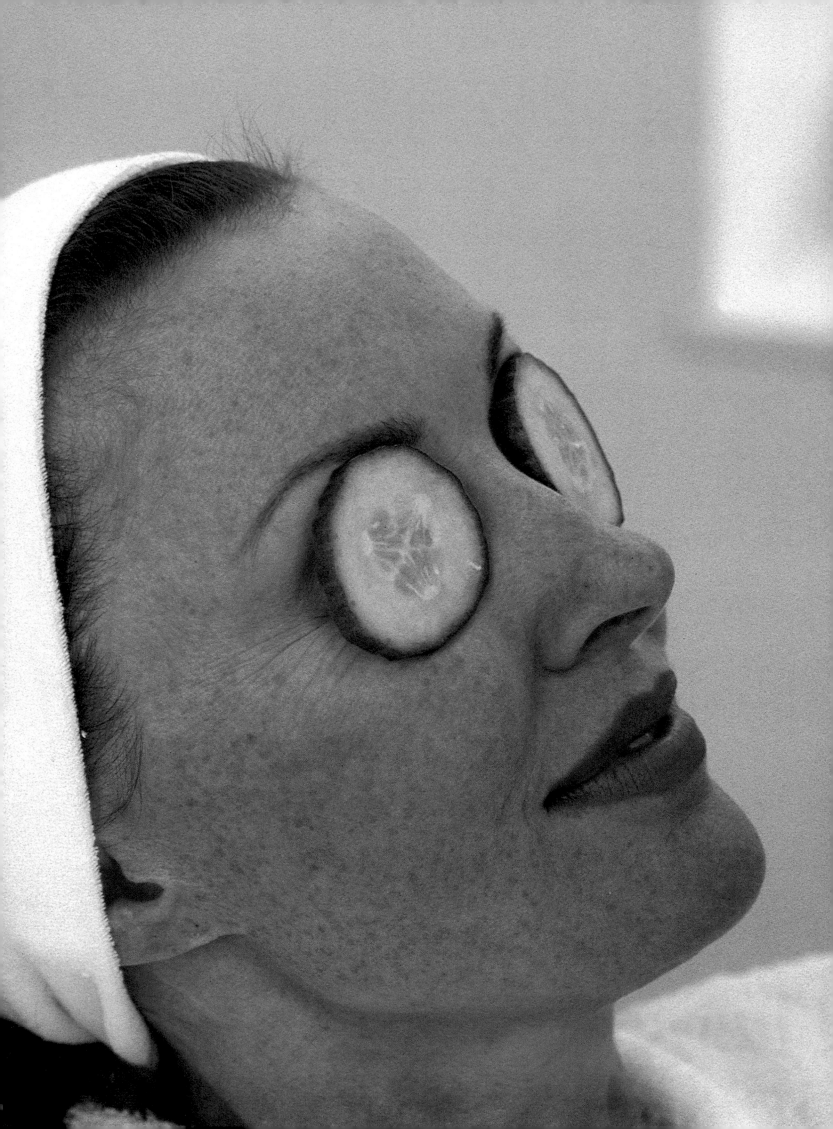

Taking care of your appearance

As you grow older the skin loses its natural elasticity and the hair becomes prone to greying and thinning — for many people these are the first visible signs of aging. There are some good techniques for preventing or accommodating changes in your appearance.

It is worth remembering that if you are happy about the way you look this has an inspiring effect on your mood, making you feel more positive, confident and sociable.

Protecting the skin

△ Add evening primrose oil or vitamin E to face cream to help rejuvinate mature skin.

The skin is our largest organ and it serves as a protective barrier against bacteria and other invaders. As you age, your skin loses its elasticity, it gets thinner and it starts to wrinkle. In fact, the appearance of the skin is one of the main criterion that we use to judge a person's age. But, although the aging process results in skin wrinkling, it is only partly responsible: ultraviolet light from the sun also plays a large role.

△ You should regularly apply a good quality cream or moisturizer to your skin to prevent the top layer of skin from drying out.

△ Skin cells contain about half the body's water content, so it is essential to maintain the fluid level for healthy skin.

△ Protecting the skin from harmful sun rays is essential in the battle against aging.

how the skin ages

A protein called collagen is responsible for keeping the skin supple, elastic and youthful. When the skin is exposed to ultraviolet light from the sun, collagen fibres are attacked and destroyed. Although you lose collagen naturally with age, exposure to the sun greatly accelerates this process (so does cigarette smoking). Ultraviolet rays also damage the layer of skin where new cells are formed. The shape of the cells changes and they become smaller. This causes the skin to lose its thickness and become more translucent. Skin ages at a different rate on different areas of the body. Two of the first places that wrinkles appear

are the hands and the face because both are constantly exposed to the elements. The skin on the neck, which is very mobile, is also prone to visible loosening and sagging with age.

Sebaceous glands, which secrete a lubricating substance onto the surface of the skin, become less active with age, resulting in dryness and flakiness.

common skin problems

Apart from wrinkling and sagging, there are some specific skin problems that are more likely to occur with age. These include broken veins and itchiness.

Broken veins become more visible as the skin ages and becomes translucent. As with age spots, broken veins do not require any special treatment. If broken veins are particularly unsightly, however, they can be removed using techniques such as electrocautery.

Itchiness of the skin may sometimes be associated with the menopause. A persistent sensation of tingling or itchiness around this time is known as formication. Some doctors recommend hormone replacement therapy (HRT) to treat this condition, as well as other menopausal symptoms.

taking care of your skin

The single most effective way to prevent premature skin aging is to protect your skin from the ultraviolet rays of the sun. This means avoiding exposure to intense sunlight whenever possible, covering your skin and wearing a sun hat on sunny days, and getting into the habit of always wearing a high protection sunscreen or sunblock.

Another way to protect your skin is to minimize free radical damage to body cells (free radicals are highly reactive substances produced during oxidation) from cigarette smoking and pollution. Avoid exposure to cigarette smoke (or quit smoking yourself) and environmental pollution, and eat foods that are rich in

△ **Eating at least five servings of fresh fruit or vegetables each day helps to encourage skin cell regeneration.**

△ **Always try to use natural oils, rather than commercially produced products, on your body.**

△ **Drinking water not only hydrates the skin but also helps to flush away toxins.**

vitamins A, C, and E, betacarotene and selenium or zinc. These nutrients help to fight free radicals in the body; you can also take them in supplement form. Skin health can also be greatly enhanced by making sure that you always have sufficient, good quality sleep.

Other dietary habits that will keep your skin youthful include the following:
- Limit your intake of tea, coffee, alcohol, sugar and saturated fat.
- Take an evening primrose oil supplement. This contains essential fatty acids that are needed by skin cell membranes.
- Drink plenty of pure water. Dehydration affects the skin and makes it dry.
- Increase the amount of fruit and vegetables in your diet, especially red, orange and yellow ones.

There are some "external" habits that you can adopt to preserve your skin. Try not to wash your skin too often and avoid harsh soaps that strip the skin of oil. Add oil to bath water and use good quality moisturizers (preferably containing sunscreen) on your body, hands and face. Moisturizers prevent the top layer of the skin from drying out but they cannot restore lost collagen.

◁ **Extremes of temperature are not good for older, thinner skin, and tepid water should be used for inhalations.**

Aromatherapy cleanser

A good cleanser to make yourself consists of 1 teaspoon of cider vinegar, 200ml/7 fl oz of purified water and one drop each of frankincense, sandalwood and lemon essential oils. Mix the ingredients and apply to the skin on cotton wool balls. For an antiseptic version, replace one of the above oils with tea tree oil.

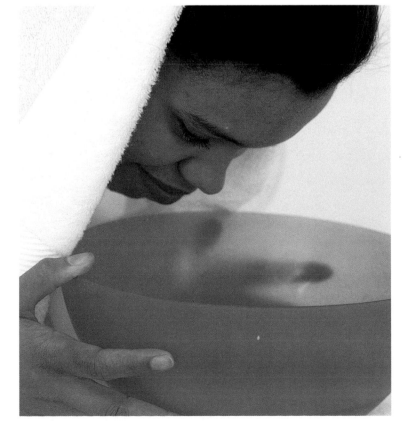

Beauty tips

Cosmetic products and procedures – and even cosmetic surgery – are frequently presented as a panacea for age-related problems. Unfortunately, they are often expensive and do not yield any long-term benefits. The alternative to shop-bought products are safe and simple techniques and practices evolved over hundreds of years from complementary therapies such as herbalism and aromatherapy.

△ For shine-free skin, blot your face with a tissue after allowing your moisturizer to sink in for five minutes.

stay moisturized

Even if moisturizers cannot restore lost skin tone, they can rehydrate the top layer of your skin, making it look firmer and healthier. To optimize absorption of moisturizer, apply it immediately after a bath when your skin is still warm and damp.

△ The back of the neck is an area often exposed to sunlight, and may require extra moisturizing.

Do not forget to moisturize your neck, an area which is a much neglected and that is prone to sun damage.

Vitamin E is an important anti-aging vitamin for the skin which can be applied externally or ingested. Massage the

▷ Applying the contents of a vitamin E capsule to your face once a week can help to soften aging skin.

△ Use lavender, peppermint and eucalyptus for an invigorating bath.

△ Calendula oil is a gentle skin reviver.

contents of a vitamin E capsule into your face or, if you prefer to include vitamin E in the foods you eat, good sources include unrefined corn oil, sunflower seeds, sesame seeds, beans, wheatgerm and tuna. Try the following recipe for

calendula (marigold) cream. Mix 55g/2oz lanolin with 50ml/2fl oz wheatgerm oil. Add a handful of fresh or dried calendula flowers and heat for approximately two hours. Strain the liquid, add two capsules of vitamin E and leave to set in a jar. Use as an everyday moisturizer.

You can also use essential oils to lubricate your skin. Use 15ml/1tbsp of a base oil, such as evening primrose or sweet almond oil, and add 1 drop of an essential oil such as frankincense, geranium, lavender, neroli (orange blossom), or sandalwood. Massage gently into the skin taking care to avoid the eyes.

take herbal baths

You can improve the way you look and feel by taking a relaxing and therapeutic herbal bath. Turn out the lights and place some lit candles around the bath. Make sure that the water is the right temperature. There are a wide variety of commercial aromatherapy and herbal products that you can add to a bath or you can try making your own. To make a herbal tea bag, place the herbs in the centre of a coffee filter. Fold it and sew the open edges closed with a needle and cotton. Alternatively, place the herbs into a piece of muslin and tie the material with ribbon.

△ Add different essential oils to your bath water to achieve calming or invigorating baths.

For a calming bath, use equal parts of camomile, hops and passion flower. For a stimulating bath, use equal parts of peppermint, eucalyptus and lavender.

Aromatherapists recommend that you add essential oils to your bath water to benefit from their therapeutic effects. For a calming bath use four drops of lavender, four drops of neroli and two drops of geranium For a stimulating bath use two drops of lemon, three drops of peppermint and three drops of rosemary.

While you are in the bath you can give your eyes a treat by covering them with cold, damp teabags, cucumber slices, or cotton wool.

have a massage

Having a regular massage is an excellent way to increase circulation, calm the nervous system, relieve muscle tension, promote

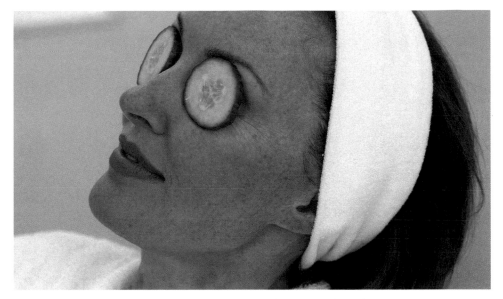

△ Make sure that you rinse cucumber slices to rid them of any pesticides before placing over your eyes.

sleep and improve posture, vitality and mood. These, in turn, have a knock on effect on your appearance. If you can, have an aromatherapy massage on a regular basis. Alternatively, give and receive a massage with a friend or partner. Simple massage strokes are easy to learn. The main strokes are effleurage, petrissage and tapotement.

•Effleurage: keep both hands flat on the skin and use long strokes in the direction of the muscle fibres. Keep hands in contact with the skin at all times and apply firm pressure to areas such as the back and buttocks; light pressure to the front of the body.

•Petrissage: use the hands in a squeezing or pinching movement across the muscle fibres. A variation of petrissage is known as friction: use the thumbs and fingers to apply circular pressure on a single spot or a series of spots.

•Tapotement: cup the hands loosely and make light hacking strokes. This is also known as percussion and works best on muscular areas of the body.

When you give a massage, you should always lubricate your hands with oil first. Avoid giving massage to people who suffer from skin problems or health problems such as osteoporosis.

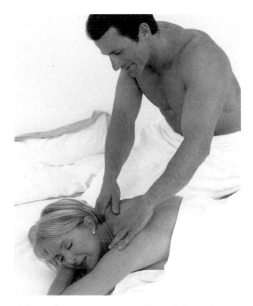

△ As well as promoting good blood circulation, massaging the body is the perfect way to apply moisturizing body oils to the skin.

A natural face pack

As your skin ages, you may find that commercial face packs strip your skin of oils, especially if they contain clay. To make a natural face pack that will help to moisturize and condition older skin, mash together half an avocado (or one raw egg yolk) with a small amount of honey. Apply to the face avoiding the eye area, and leave on for approximately 10 minutes. Use this face pack every week.

Pampered hands

△ Light nail polishes and shorter nails are more flattering for older hands.

Hands are a good indication of the state of the body and many therapists use them as diagnostic tools when judging general health. Dry or brittle nails, for example, may reveal a lack of B vitamins, white flecks may indicate a lack of zinc, and weak nails may indicate calcium deficiency. The skin on the backs of the hands indicates a person's age.

how the hands age

As you age, the skin on your hands tends to become dry and fragile, the nails may thicken and become ridged or they may get brittle and prone to breaking. Veins become more pronounced, age spots appear and the hand becomes thinner and less fleshy.

common hand problems

As you grow older it is common for age spots to appear on the backs of the hands. Age spots, sometimes known as liver spots, are due to melanin-producing cells clumping together with age. Melanin is a pigment produced by the skin that gives rise to the characteristic brown colour of a suntan. When melanin-producing cells clump together they produce distinctive brown spots or patches. Although age spots are not thought to be harmful, they can be

△ You should try to remember to moisturize your hands at least twice a day.

removed using laser or chemical treatment. Massaging the hands with saffron oil may also be helpful.

Age spots may be worsened by cold weather and exposure to the ultraviolet rays of the sun, so always wear sunscreen on the hands in summer and gloves in winter.

Arthritis can cause problems such as pain, restricted movement and dexterity and

△ A few drops of lemon juice mixed into yogurt can help reduce age spots.

Skin aging on the hands

The backs of the hands are often the first place where skin starts to age. Try pinching the skin on the back of your hand for a few seconds and then release it. The rate at which it falls back into place varies according to age.

Under 30: 1 second

30–40 years: 1–2 seconds

40–50 years: 2–5 seconds

50–60 years: 10–15 seconds

even disfigurement in the hands as you grow older. Arthritis should receive medical diagnosis and treatment, but self-help measures include taking painkillers and applying alternate hot or cold compresses to the hands. Hand massage can also be helpful.

To give a massage, lubricate your hands with base oil mixed with a few drops of marjoram essential oil and gently sandwich one of the sufferer's hands in between both of yours. Gently stroke the length of the hand from the wrist to the fingertips. The warmth of your hands will ease the pain. Now gently rub and stroke the thumb.

△ **1** After removing all traces of nail polish, soak your nails in warm olive oil for ten minutes.

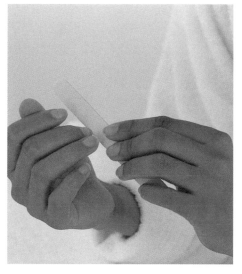

△ **2** To file your nails use a padded emery board. Sweep from the outer corner inward to avoid splitting the nails.

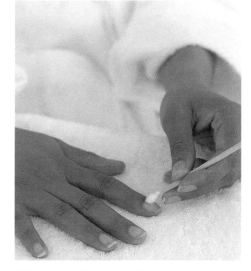

△ **3** Push your cuticles back with an orange stick wrapped in cotton wool.

looking after your hands

Moisturize your hands as often as possible, but at least once in the morning and evening, and after immersing your hands in water. Moisturizer is absorbed into the skin most quickly when it is warm, so apply it to warm hands or keep a bottle near to a source of heat.

Cleaning dishes in hot water that contains detergent can take its toll on your hands over many years. A good way to prevent skin damage is to cover your hands in handcream and put rubber gloves on before washing up. The warmth of the water will enhance the skin's absorption of the moisturizer.

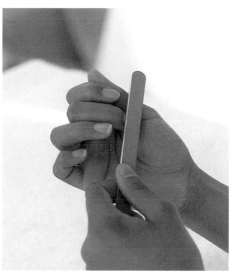

△ **4** Buffing your nails will gently smooth away hard surface ridges.

Once a week, soak your fingertips in warm olive oil (or cider vinegar if you have weak nails) for 10 minutes. Then gently rub a teaspoon of salt into your hands. The abrasive action of the salt will remove dead skin cells. Now trim your nails using a pair of nail scissors, and file them into shape. Use an emery board and sweep from the outer corner of the nail inwards. Push the cuticles back with an orange stick wrapped in cotton wool. Now buff your nails to smooth away ridges and give them a natural shine.

Always try to wear at least a clear nail polish to protect your nails against everyday wear and tear. If you are applying a coloured nail varnish, always use an undercoat first to prevent the pigment from sinking into the nails and causing staining. A top coat can double the length of time required between manicures by preventing chipping.

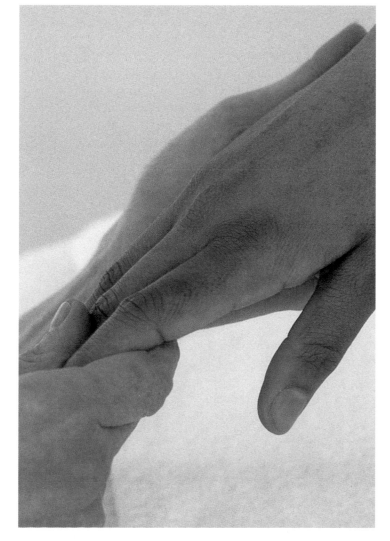

◁ **Add a teaspoon of salt to warm olive oil and massage well into the hands to remove dead skin cells (use cider vinegar instead of oil if the nails are weak).**

Foot care

Years of wear and tear combined with badly fitting or poorly designed shoes can have an adverse effect on the feet as you grow older. You can also add to the burden by trimming the toenails badly or neglecting problems such as dry skin, corns and bunions. Good foot care is an important investment in your mobility – present and future.

common foot complaints

Corns and calluses are caused by friction between shoes and the bony areas of the foot. The bony parts of the foot become less padded with age, making corns and calluses more likely. Prevention consists of wearing padded insoles, padding vulnerable areas of the feet and wearing well-fitting shoes. You can treat corns and calluses using over-the-counter medication.

Ingrown toenails occur when the toenail pierces the skin of the foot, and are most common on the big toes. This problem is

△ Achilles tendons may shorten due to prolonged wearing of heels. Try to go barefoot or in flat slippers for at least two hours a day to allow the tendons to stretch to their full length.

◁ To assist against perspiring feet add 4 drops each of bergamot and clary sage and 2 drops of cypress essential oil to a footbath.

usually caused by trimming the toenails in the wrong way. To prevent ingrown toenails, always cut the nail square across and level with the top of the toe. Never taper the sides of the nails or poke scissors or other implements underneath the nail. If you suspect that you have an ingrown toenail, visit a doctor or chiropodist (podiatrist). Treatment involves cutting away the part of the nail that is breaking the skin and protecting the area as it heals.

Bunions are painful and severely retard mobility. They are caused by the overgrowth of bone tissue, and although the problem is

▷ To nourish the skin add a handful of dried milk to a warm footbath and soak feet for 15 minutes.

often hereditary, it can be exacerbated by wearing ill-fitting shoes. A bunion is characterized by a swollen, tender big toe joint that protrudes from the foot. In mild cases, the bunion can be accommodated by wearing wide-fitting shoes or a protective pad on the toe joint. In severe cases, the foot can become misaligned and medical attention is necessary. Your doctor may recommend drug treatment or surgery.

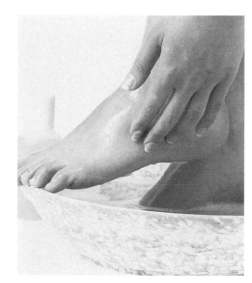

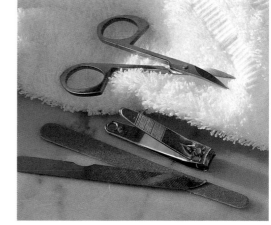

◁ Add a few drops of peppermint essential oil to baby oil and massage to relieve tired feet.

▷ Always make sure you cut your toe nails straight across to avoid ingrowing nails.

▽ Regular use of a pumice stone after bathing can stop hard skin building up and causing problems.

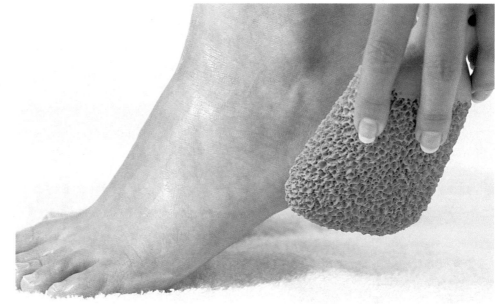

Skin cracking around the heel is very common with age. An easy self-help treatment is to soak your feet in warm water, then cover them with petroleum jelly, and put on a pair of cotton socks before going to bed. You can also alleviate dry skin by increasing the amount of essential fatty acids in your diet. Essential fatty acids are found in extra virgin olive oil, sunflower seeds and oily fish. You may also benefit from taking a vitamin E supplement or a tablespoon of linseed oil every day. If cracking is severe, dietary therapists may recommend taking 30mg of zinc twice a day over an eight-week period.

Even if you do not suffer from cracked skin, moisturize your feet after bathing. Skin on the foot is drier than elsewhere on the body, so try to use specially designed foot

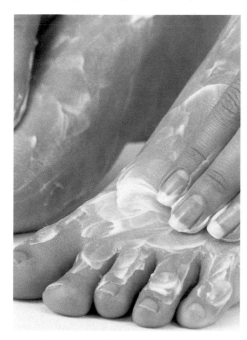

△ Moisturizing the feet regularly not only helps to prevent dry skin, but by massaging the creams in, you can promote healthy circulation.

care products. If your feet sweat excessively, soak them in a bowl of warm water mixed with a handful of dried milk instead of applying moisturizer. Another useful remedy for dry, tired feet is a few drops of peppermint oil added to some baby lotion.

looking after your feet

Babies are born with fat, padded feet, but as you grow and your bones form, the feet become leaner and more defined. As you age the padding on the feet lessens still further and the feet become wider. Because your feet change throughout life, it is essential to have your feet measured periodically so that you can buy shoes that fit correctly. Choose socks that are the right size for your feet and whenever you have the chance, go barefoot. Another aspect of good foot care is a regular visit to a chiropodist (podiatrist).

The following tips can help to maintain the health of the feet and prevent problems.
• Give yourself a foot massage using essential oils mixed with a base oil.
• Avoid exposure to cold temperatures.

• Make sure that your socks do not impede circulation.
• Avoid sitting with one leg crossed over the other.
• Promote circulation by flexing and pointing your toes and circling your ankles, especially if you sit still for long periods of time.
• Sit with your feet raised whenever possible.
• Treat your feet to a warm foot bath and apply a special foot moisturizer afterwards.

Footcare for diabetics

The feet are particularly vulnerable to infection in people who suffer from diabetes (adult-onset diabetes becomes more common as you age). If you have diabetes, pay careful attention to foot care and consult your doctor about any foot problems, even minor ones such as corns and calluses. Avoid self-help treatment and visit a chiropodist regularly.

Healthy hair

As we age our hair tends to get thinner and turn grey. These tangible signs of aging are ones that many people try to prevent or conceal. As a result we spend much time and money on styling, colouring, treating and transplanting hair. Ultimately, many age-related hair changes are hard to prevent because they are genetically controlled. But this does not prevent us from having hair that is healthy and attractive.

△ **After shampooing, rinse your hair with warm water until the water runs clear and clean.**

△ **Having a fringe is flattering on older people as it can often soften their appearance as well as help to hide forehead lines.**

how the hair ages

On average we lose between 70 and 100 hairs per day. When we are young we replace these lost hairs with new ones but, as we grow older, hair loss speeds up and new growth slows down. Some hair follicles become sluggish and have long resting phases, other hair follicles appear to be completely deactivated. The result of these changes is fewer hairs and the overall appearance of thinning. Women may notice that their hair starts to thin out around the time of the menopause. However, if you suffer from sudden or severe hair loss, consult your doctor.

Men are prone to a particular type of hair thinning known as "male pattern baldness". This is distinct from age-related thinning and it is genetically controlled. Hair follicles that are affected by male pattern baldness start to produce a new type of hair known as a vellus hair. These are thin and delicate and they only grow to a short length. Because they are difficult to see, vellus hairs may give the impression of baldness. Eventually, true baldness occurs as the follicles die completely. Men can usually predict whether they will go bald simply by looking at older male members of their family. Although men may suffer from thinning

and baldness of head hair, they may find that nasal and eyebrow hair begins to grow more vigorously with age.

Hair that turns grey does so because of the loss of a pigment called melanin. As a hair shaft is produced, the hair follicle secretes melanin giving hair its characteristic colour. As pigment cells start to die – but some melanin is still produced – the hair has a grey colour. When the pigment cells die completely, the hair is white. Unpigmented hair has a characteristic coarse, wiry texture. Many people start to develop grey hairs in their 30s and 40s and hair becomes progressively more grey with age.

△ Use as few chemicals as possible, instead opt for natural products such as sesame conditioner.

looking after your hair

The key to having attractive and healthy hair as you get older is to wear it in a style that suits you and to keep it in optimum condition. This does not mean buying expensive hair products; in fact, the major determinants of hair health are regular exercise, a well-balanced diet and adequate sleep.

- Grey hair can be concealed with temporary or permanent colouring. Choose a shade that is lighter than your original colour. You may need to experiment with different products – the way in which your hair responds to colorants depends on how porous your hair shafts are.
- To condition dry, brittle hair, boil 3 tablespoons of ground sesame seeds in a little water for 10 minutes, strain through muslin and allow to cool. Massage the mixture into the hair and leave for 10 minutes before rinsing thoroughly.

▷ Always gently comb conditioner through the hair to ensure it is evenly distributed and reaches as many hairs as possible.

- Aromatherapists recommend the following tonic to revitalize hair: mix 10 drops of cedarwood essential oil, 10 drops of juniper essential oil and 15 drops of rosemary essential oil in 50ml/2fl oz of surgical spirit (alcohol). Massage a small amount of this mixture into damp hair and leave to dry naturally. Wash your hands afterwards.
- Dietary therapists recommend eliminating coffee, tea and sugar from the diet in order to promote hair health. Useful nutrients include essential fatty acids for dry or brittle hair, zinc for poor hair growth and a general multivitamin and mineral supplement for overall hair health.
- Avoid drying out your hair using hot hair dryers or styling tools, and try not to use bleach – it strips the hair of natural oils. Use an intensive conditioning treatment on your hair once a month.

Menopausal changes to hair

Oestrogen receptors are present in hair follicles and when oestrogen levels fall at the time of the menopause the growth and rest cycle of the hair is disrupted. Many women notice for the first time that their hair is thin, fine and difficult to style. This change is completely natural. Although you cannot reverse hormonally-related hair thinning (except with hormone replacement therapy) you can help to minimize hair loss by treating your hair gently. When you wash your hair, mix a mild shampoo with some water and then pour the mixture over your head. Leave it for a minute and then massage very gently and rinse off with warm water. Dab your hair rather than rubbing and comb with a wide-toothed comb. Leave your hair to dry naturally.

◁ Herbal hair rinses use natural ingredients to leave your hair shining and well conditioned.

▷ Comb wet hair with a wide-toothed comb to gently free any tangles.

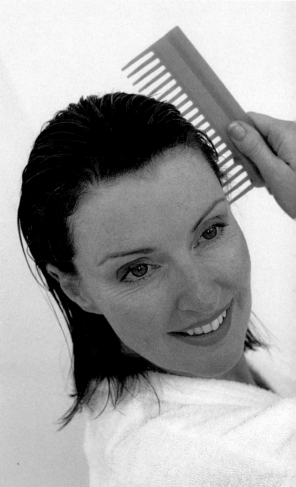

Menopause

The menopause is the permanent cessation of the menstrual cycle, bringing to a close the period of life in which it was possible to bear children.

It usually occurs between the ages of 45 and 50, although both early and late menopause are not unusual. While the prospect of the menopause may seem daunting, you should try to not to worry unduly. You can reduce the likelihood of suffering physical or psychological problems by adopting a positive attitude towards this new stage in your life.

The changing menstrual cycle

To understand what happens during menopause, it is important to know about the sequence of finely tuned hormonal events that takes place in the normal menstrual cycle.

the menstrual cycle

At the beginning of every menstrual cycle, a hormone is released from the brain called follicle-stimulating hormone (FSH). It stimulates the development of egg follicles in the ovary. As the follicles develop they produce the hormone oestrogen. One egg follicle eventually becomes dominant and releases an egg – a process known as ovulation – which travels down the fallopian tube. The follicle that produced the egg is left behind on the ovary where it starts to secrete the hormone progesterone.

As the egg travels down along the fallopian tube, the uterus, under hormonal direction, is preparing itself for a possible pregnancy. Oestrogen makes the uterine lining thicken and progesterone stimulates the growth of blood vessels so that the uterus is ready to receive a fertilized egg. If fertilization does not happen then the egg and uterine lining are simply shed from the body in a process known as menstruation.

In most healthy young women, the menstrual cycle takes place on a fairly regular basis – about every 28 days on

△ Irregular periods may be stabilized by adding 4 drops each of rose, camomile and melissa to a warm bath.

average. Several factors can change or disrupt the menstrual cycle, such as stress, illness, losing an excessive amount of weight or taking the contraceptive pill. The biggest changes, however, come with menopause.

changes to the cycle

As women grow older the brain releases follicle-stimulating hormone (FSH) in the way that it always has done, but the ovary does not respond in the usual way. With age there are less follicles left in the ovary to be stimulated, and the ones that remain may be of insufficient quality to make it to ovulation. This has several results: the brain increases the amount of FSH to "force" the ovary to respond, the remaining follicles

◁ The menopause usually occurs between the ages of 45 and 50, although both early and late menopause are not unsual.

△ **Regular exercise helps keep the body in balance by regulating body fluids and reducing fluid retention.**

produce less oestrogen than normal and, if ovulation does not happen, no progesterone is secreted.

These are the kinds of disruptions that take place in the menstrual cycle during the build up to the menopause. Ultimately, oestrogen levels go into permanent decline and ovulation becomes erratic and ceases, causing progesterone production and periods to stop as well.

the menopause timetable

Menopausal changes rarely happen suddenly. They usually take place over years. You may notice that your periods become more frequent and longer in duration. Or you may notice that your periods become infrequent with less blood loss than usual. Or you may alternate between both patterns. It is difficult to know what to expect. Some women skip periods for several months and then suddenly start menstruating again.

The word "menopause" refers to a single event rather than a series of ongoing changes: it is a woman's last ever menstrual period. This cannot be identified when it is happening – it can only be identified retrospectively. A more accurate word to describe the ongoing hormonal changes of midlife is the "perimenopause". Or some doctors use the word "climacteric". The postmenopause describes the years between the last period and the end of a woman's life.

• Premenopause: periods are still regular but symptoms may start to appear.
• Perimenopause: periods become unpredictable and symptoms may worsen.
• Postmenopause: periods stop permanently and, in time, the body adjusts to low hormone levels.

the age of menopause

Most women become menopausal in their 40s and 50s. The average age of menopause is about 51 years, although perimenopausal signs may be apparent before this age. Premature menopause takes place before the age of 35 and delayed menopause takes place after the age of 55.

It is likely that, as individuals, we are biologically programmed to reach menopause at a certain age. There is no link between the age of menopause and age of first menstruation or first pregnancy. Taking

△ **Practising relaxation exercises can help to harmonize your body and alleviate symptoms of the menopause.**

the contraceptive pill is not thought to influence the age of menopause. The age at which your mother was menopausal may affect the age of your menopause, but this is not conclusive. Smoking and low body weight, however, have been found to bring on the menopause earlier.

▽ **The more positive an outlook you have on life, the fewer physical and psychological problems are likely to occur at the time of the menopause.**

Symptoms of the menopause

Although some women experience very few problems at menopause, others begin to experience an array of symptoms that affect both the body and mind. One of the main reasons for this is the fact that oestrogen influences many different body functions. In fact, special receptor cells for oestrogen are present all over the body and in the brain.

why the menopause causes symptoms

Some experts have compared the symptoms of oestrogen decline to drug withdrawal: when supplies of oestrogen start to become erratic the body reacts negatively; if oestrogen levels are restored, the body gets its "fix" and returns to normal. Eventually, the body adapts to low oestrogen levels but this is something that may take years. Problems may also result from the fact that hormones released in the brain such as follicle stimulating hormone (FSH) can become unusually high.

Much research focuses on the importance of oestrogen but it is now thought that progesterone (or its absence) may also be important. After menopause, progesterone production stops completely whereas small amounts of oestrogen are still produced (fat cells produce oestrogen). This relative imbalance, coupled with progesterone deficiency, is thought to be a cause of troubling symptoms.

Warning signs
Menstrual upheavals are common around the time of the menopause but you should consult your doctor if you experience any of the following:
- Bleeding between periods
- Heavy bleeding with clots
- Bleeding after sex
- Bleeding following a year without periods

Common symptoms
Symptoms are many and varied as the hormone levels in the body fluctuate. Some of the most common symptoms are:
- Hot flushes and night sweats
- Palpitations
- Breast changes
- Mood swings
- Depression
- Poor memory
- Insomnia
- Tiredness
- Poor concentration
- Loss of sex drive
- Vaginal dryness
- Urinary problems
- Fluid retention
- Weight gain and shape change

▽ **Wearing cotton clothes, drinking iced water and using a battery-operated fan can help to ease the symptoms of hot flushes.**

hot flushes and night sweats

The most easily identifiable symptoms of the menopause are hot flushes and night sweats. Blood rushes to the face, neck and chest and you become hot, flushed and sweaty. Afterwards you may feel very cold. This can happen very frequently, sometimes several times an hour. When it happens at night, you may wake up drenched in sweat and feeling hot and feverish. Self-help measures:

- Find effective ways of cooling down. Carry a battery-operated fan or an insulated flask of iced water with you.
- Wear cotton or other natural fibres.
- Wear clothes that can be unbuttoned at the neck.
- Keep a record of when you have hot flushes and see if you can recognize a pattern. Are there any specific triggers?
- Avoid spicy food, caffeine and alcohol.
- Learn to relax and practise creative visualization techniques.

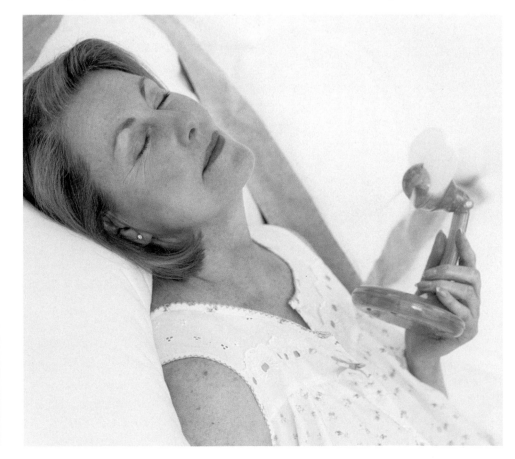

palpitations

Many women experience palpitations at the same time as they have a hot flush. However, they can also appear independently of hot flushes. The heart feels as though it is racing or beating irregularly and some women feel as though they are having a panic attack. Self-help measures:

• Take a break and sit or lie down.
• Close your eyes, inhale deeply through your nose and take the breath down into your abdomen.
• Tell yourself that the feeling is temporary and will soon pass.

△ **Aromatherapists recommend the use of clary sage against hot flushes and night sweats.**

△ **St John's Wort, recommended for lifting depression and stabilizing mood swings, can be taken as a tea, a tincture or a supplement.**

◁ **Keep a diary of menopausal symptoms – there may be a pattern to hot flushes and palpitations.**

▷ **Creating a relaxing atmosphere can help to ease palpitations, mood swings and depression.**

breast changes

The most common type of menopausal breast change is mastalgia. The breasts typically feel swollen, tender and painful to the touch. Self-help measures:

• Wear a good quality bra that supports your breasts. Wear a bra in bed if necessary.
• Cut down on the amount of saturated fat that you eat.

mood swings and depression

Fluctuating hormone levels may give rise to emotional problems such as irritability, crying fits, angry outbursts and anxiety. This is because oestrogen receptors in the parts of the brain that control mood are deprived of oestrogen. Disrupted sleep due to night sweats may give rise to mood swings. Feeling tired all the time will lessen your ability to cope. Self-help measures:

• Seek the support of your friends, family and partner. Explain to them how you are feeling.
• Talk to other menopausal women about their feelings or read the experiences of others. Join a self-help group.
• Learn relaxation and mood-lifting techniques that work for you.
• Try taking flower remedies or herbal remedies such as St. John's wort or kava kava (stop if you experience any side effects and if you are taking prescribed medications, consult your doctor).

More menopausal symptoms

poor memory

Forgetfulness often becomes a problem around the time of menopause. You may find yourself missing appointments or forgetting where you put things. The hippocampus, the part of the brain that is associated with memory, contains oestrogen receptors and may be less efficient at storing information when oestrogen levels start to decline.
Self-help measures:

- Teach yourself to rely on diaries and lists. Keep exhaustive lists of everything that you need to remember.
- Keep a pen and a piece of paper by your bed and in your car.
- Highlight the most essential daily tasks that you must do. Tick them off at the end of the day.

△ Keep a pen and paper beside the bed so that you can easily jot down important things that you remember during the night.

insomnia

The inability to fall asleep, waking frequently during the night and waking up too early are all classified as signs of insomnia. Suffering from insomnia may be a menopausal symptom in its own right or it may be caused by night sweats.

△ Massage relaxes the muscles and releases sleep-inducing chemicals in the brain.

tiredness

Feeling sleepy, apathetic or fatigued during the day can exacerbate other menopausal symptoms such as poor memory and concentration. Muscle fatigue is common during the menopause. Self-help measures:

- Accept your limitations: if you feel tired, try to rest rather than keep going.
- Avoid artificial stimulants such as coffee, chocolate and alcohol.
- Practise good sleeping habits (see Looking after the body).

poor concentration

Like poor memory, poor concentration is another cognitive deficit caused by declining or fluctuating levels of oestrogen in the body. Some people also find decision making more difficult than previously.

Self-help measures:

- Be lenient on yourself. Find out what your attention span is and work around it.
- Do not resign yourself to diminishing brain power. Stay mentally active.

loss of sex drive

Women notice that their sex drive decreases or even disappears around the time of menopause. This may happen spontaneously or it may be the result of an underlying problem such as vaginal dryness, breast pain, tiredness or depression.
Self-help measures:

- Establish the underlying cause of the problem and, if possible, treat it.
- Remember that sex does not always have to be penetrative. Try being sexually intimate with a partner by cuddling or

giving each other a massage.
- Remember that postmenopausal women often experience renewed sexual interest.

vaginal dryness

Declining levels of oestrogen cause the urogenital tract to become thin and dry. The vaginal tissues shrink and less lubrication is produced than previously. This can make sex difficult and painful. Menopausal women may also be prone to vaginal soreness and minor infection.

Self-help measures:
- Insert a vitamin E capsule into the vagina nightly for a month and then whenever you need to.
- Use a natural lubricating gel, such as aloe vera or comfrey cream.
- Spend longer on foreplay during sex – the vagina may just be slower to lubricate than before.
- You should try and remain sexually active, as this will keep your reproductive system in good shape.

urinary problems

The urinary tract lies very close to the vagina and it also responds to declining oestrogen levels by becoming thin. The result of this may be discomfort on passing urine and frequent and urgent urination. Some women suffer from stress incontinence in which small amounts of urine escape from the body on laughing,

coughing or picking up a heavy object.
Self-help measures:
- Drink 2 litres/3½ pints of water a day to keep the bladder flushed out.
- Practise Kegel exercises. These involve tensing the pelvic floor muscles (those used to stop urination) for a count of five. Repeat throughout the day.

fluid retention

A common feature of premenstrual syndrome, fluid retention, can become worse in the build-up to the menopause. You may feel bloated, swollen and heavy. If your weight fluctuates substantially, you should seek a professional diagnosis as you may have developed a food intolerance.
Self-help measures:
- Cut out salt, processed food and junk food.
- Eat foods that act as natural diuretics such as celery, parsley, chicory and dandelion.
- Avoid standing for long periods.
- Take plenty of exercise.

weight gain and shape change

Many women find that they put on weight during the menopause due to a lowered metabolism and a change in the way that fat is deposited in the body. Long-term low oestrogen levels also cause the body to change shape. The waist-to-hip ratio alters so that the waist thickens and comes out to meet the hips.

Self-help measures:
- Avoid faddish diets and calorie restriction at the time of the menopause. You need calcium and all the other nutrients that a normal diet supplies.
- Use exercise to control your weight and increase muscle tone.

△ **Natural diuretics such as celery, chicory, parsley and dandelion can help fight against fluid retention.**

▽ **Tightening and relaxing the muscles used to stop urination helps to prevent stress and incontinence.**

hormone replacement therapy

Hormone replacement therapy (HRT) is a type of medication that is designed to return a menopausal women's hormone levels back to her premenopausal levels. Doctors often prescribe HRT to treat debilitating menopausal symptoms such as hot flushes, insomnia and depression. HRT may also have a role in protecting women against the long-term health problems that are most frequently associated with the postmenopause such as osteoporosis and cardiovascular disease.

what is HRT?

HRT consists of the hormones oestrogen and progestogen (the synthetic form of progesterone). Oestrogen is widely considered to be the most important hormone in HRT; the role of progestogen is to induce a monthly bleed and to protect the uterus from cancer. Women who have had a hysterectomy may be prescribed oestrogen only.

The main advantage of HRT is that it may reverse many of the changes associated with menopause. This means that premenopausal body shape, skin and hair condition, sex drive and cardiovascular health can all be preserved and the classic menopausal symptoms are alleviated. The disadvantages are that women continue to bleed on a monthly basis (this is a withdrawal bleed rather than a proper period) and that HRT can cause side effects. HRT is also unsuitable for some women because of their medical history.

Some women feel that the menopause is medicalized in Western cultures and that taking medication during this time simply adds to the perception that the menopause is an illness or disease. This is a matter for debate: some people argue that women are suffering from a hormone deficiency disease that deserves medical treatment; others say that menopause is a natural rite of passage and the view that women are ill should not be encouraged.

types of HRT

HRT is usually taken in pill form. The pills often come in calendar packs and you take one pill a day. All the pills usually contain oestrogen, whereas progestogen is only included in 10–14 pills in the latter half of the pill cycle.

Hormones can be absorbed through the skin and are available in the form of skin patches. The fact that hormones do not have to pass through the liver means

△ **Weight bearing exercise can help to prevent osteoporosis, as well as promote good circulation.**

that dosages are comparatively low and this may be an advantage for some women. The patches should be changed every three or four days.

HRT is also available in implant form. The implant is inserted under the skin in a minor surgical procedure carried out by your doctor. Although implants are convenient, in that you do not need to take pills or change patches, it is difficult to control the dosage. Localized symptoms of low oestrogen levels, such as vaginal dryness, may be treated with oestrogen cream or pessaries. However, this form of HRT does not ease other menopausal symptoms, such as hot flushes, and it does not have the long-term benefits of other types of HRT.

the possible side effects

It may take the body a while to adjust to the hormones in HRT and some women find that they are troubled by side effects even after several months of taking hormones. There are lots of different types, products, doses and regimes in hormonal medication and, ideally, HRT should be tailored to suit every woman's individual needs. If you are taking HRT and you experience side effects, consult your doctor about trying a different brand or type of HRT or changing the dose or regime. It may be necessary for you to take HRT for at least four months before your body adapts.

Your doctor may decide that HRT is not appropriate for you if you have any of the following:

• High blood pressure
• Endometriosis (in which the lining of the uterus grows outside the uterus)
• Benign breast disease, such as cysts
• Benign uterus disease, such as fibroids
• A history of thrombosis
• Migraine
• Ovarian or uterine cancer
• Pancreatic disease
• Liver disease
• Recent cardiovascular disease
• Breast cancer or a family history of breast cancer.

Research shows that taking oestrogen and progestogen may be associated with an increased risk of breast cancer. This does not rule out taking HRT altogether but the risks and benefits for each woman need to be assessed carefully by a doctor.

▷ **You should discuss any menopausal symptoms with your doctor to make sure that you receive the advice and treatment that you require during the menopause.**

Side effects of HRT

Some women may find that they suffer from side effects while taking HRT. These side effects may include:
• Headaches
• Nausea
• Impaired eyesight
• Breathlessness
• Premenstrual syndrome
• Heavy or irregular bleeding
• Breast tenderness
• Skin problems such as acne and itchiness
• Weight gain
• An increased or decreased sexual drive
• Muscular pains and backache

▷ **Some women find HRT patches more beneficial than tablets. Since the hormone does not have to travel through the liver, side effects are reduced.**

Natural alternatives to HRT

More and more women are turning to complementary therapies to help them through the menopausal years. A range of therapies offer gentle but effective ways to overcome symptoms and increase overall well-being. Although many therapies can be practised safely in the home, it can be helpful to seek the guidance of a therapist, at least in the first instance.

herbalism

There are many herbal treatments for menopausal symptoms and the best advice is to visit a medical herbalist who will tailor treatments to your individual needs. Herbal remedies come in a variety of forms including infusions, decoctions and tinctures – these can be made with fresh or dried herbs. There are also many commercial herbal supplements in the form of pills or capsules that are available in health food shops or some pharmacies.

Herbs that contain oestrogen-like substances – known as phyto-oestrogens – may compensate for declining oestrogen levels at menopause and ease many menopausal symptoms. Such herbs include panax ginseng, black cohosh, dong quai, alfalfa, liquorice and red clover. Remedies that are recommended for specific menopausal symptoms are as follows:
• Hot flushes and night sweats: agnus castus, sage, yarrow, motherwort

• Poor memory or concentration: ginkgo biloba
• Depression: St John's wort
• Anxiety: vervain
• Breast pain and pre-menstrual syndrome: evening primrose oil
• Insomnia: valerian, passionflower

Stop taking herbs if you experience any side effects. Consult your doctor before taking herbs if you suffer from high blood pressure or cardiovascular disease.

aromatherapy

The essential oils that are therapeutic at the menopause include sage, camomile, geranium, rose, jasmine, neroli, ylang ylang, bergamot and sandalwood. You can use these essential oils in the bath, in a massage (mixed with a base oil), you can burn them in an aromatherapy burner or you can put a few drops on a tissue or a pillow. Sage essential oil is thought to be good for hot flushes and ylang ylang is recommended for reviving the libido.

flower remedies

There is a wide choice of flower remedies available and you do not need to consult an expert before taking them. There is a range of flower remedies to suit various emotions and you can combine remedies to achieve the mixture that is right for your specific emotional symptoms.

homeopathy

A homeopath can assess your symptoms and choose the most suitable remedy and potency for you. Health food shops and some pharmacies also sell a standard range of homeopathic remedies. The remedies that are most frequently recommended for menopausal symptoms are as follows:
• Hot flushes: Lachesis, Sepia, Belladonna
• Breast pain: Bryonia
• Mood swings and irritability: Lachesis, Sepia, Pulsatilla
• Insomnia: Pulsatilla
• Premenstrual syndrome: Bryonia, Pulsatilla
• Vaginal dryness: Sepia, Natrum muriaticum

traditional Chinese medicine

Practitioners of Chinese medicine aim to restore the flow of energy, or Qi, through the body using acupuncture, acupressure and Chinese herbalism. Both herbs and acupuncture may be recommended for hot flushes. Always consult a registered doctor of Chinese medicine.

massage

Receiving massage can have a relaxing and therapeutic effect on both the mind and the body. If possible, visit a massage therapist and explain your symptoms. Regular massage can help to relieve insomnia, anxiety, depression and muscle and joint pain.

△ Sprinkle alfalfa shoots onto salads for a tasty and nutritious source of phyto-oestrogens.

△ The storage methods for herbs can vary greatly so always read the instructions carefully.

△ Essential oils, such as sandalwood, clary sage, or camomile, can have an uplifting effect.

yoga

A core benefit of yoga during the menopause is that it teaches you relaxation techniques that you can use at any time in your day-to-day life. The practice of breathing techniques (pranayama) can still the mind and relieve stress and anxiety. Meditation can also be of great benefit. The physical postures of yoga (asanas) can help to maintain flexibility and strength in the joints and muscles and bring balance to the body and mind. If possible, join a class and learn yoga from an experienced teacher.

△ **This yoga position, known as the Child's pose, is an excellent relaxer for the body and mind.**

dietary therapy

Research suggests that Asian women do not suffer as badly as Western women from menopausal problems and this is believed to be due to their soya-based diet, rich in phyto-oestrogens and calcium. It is worth experimenting by drinking two glasses of soya milk per day for a period of a month to see if you experience a lessening of symptoms. Other foodstuffs rich in phyto-oestrogens include oats, barley, wild rice, brown rice, wholewheat, celery (which is also useful against fluid retention), sprouts and green beans. Recommended supplements during menopause include evening primrose oil, vitamin C with bioflavonoids, vitamin E, and a general multivitamin and mineral supplement.

It is advisable to avoid the following in your diet around the time of the menopause:
• Caffeine
• Hot spicy foods
• Alcohol
• High sugar consumption
• High salt consumption
• High animal fat consumption
• Bran-based foods that may strip the body of nutrients such as calcium.

"Natural HRT" cake (7 day supply)
The following recipe for a natural HRT cake contains ingredients that are rich in phyto-oestrogens and vitamin E. It is low in fat and high in fibre and may help to alleviate symptoms of the menopause.

115g/4oz soya flour
115g/4oz wholewheat flour
115g/4oz porridge oats
5cm/2in chopped stem ginger
2.5ml/$\frac{1}{2}$ tsp ground ginger
2.5ml/$\frac{1}{2}$ tsp nutmeg
2.5ml/$\frac{1}{2}$ tsp cinnamon
200g/7oz raisins
115g/4oz linseeds
50g/2oz sunflower seeds
50g/2oz sesame seeds
50g/2oz sliced almonds
15ml/1tbsp malt extract
150 ml/$\frac{1}{4}$ pint soya milk

Sift the flour and add all the dry ingredients. Mix well before slowly adding the milk and malt extract. Cover and leave to soak for an hour. Spoon mixture into a cake tin lined with waxed paper and bake for up to 75 minutes on 190°C/370°F/gas 5. Allow to cool and eat one slice per day.

△ **Store your HRT cake in an airtight container, and eat within seven days.**

△ **You should always wash fresh fruit and vegetables thoroughly before eating in order to rinse off any traces of pesticides.**

Essential nutrient guide for the menopause
Take plenty of the following:
• Phyto-oestrogens: replace your usual milk and flour with soya milk and flour.
• Selenium-rich foods: wheatgerm, wheatbran, tuna, tomatoes and onions.
• Vitamin E-rich foods: sunflower oil, sun-dried tomatoes, seeds, almonds, unsalted peanuts, leafy green vegetables and eggs.
• Calcium-rich foods: tofu, cheese, leafy green vegetables, root vegetables, nuts and salmon.
• Magnesium-rich foods: brown rice, nuts, wholegrains and legumes.
• Potassium-rich foods: avocados, leafy green vegetables, bananas, nuts and potatoes.
• Zinc-rich foods: meat, mushrooms, eggs, wholegrains, nuts and seeds.
• Foods rich in vitamin B-complex: wholegrains, brown rice, milk, cereals, leafy green vegetables, fish, meat, eggs, avocados, seeds and yogurt.
• Vitamin D-rich foods: oily fish such as sardines, mackerel and tuna (vitamin D can also be obtained from exposure to bright sunlight).
• Water, juices and herbal teas to keep the body sufficiently hydrated.

Health checks

You should start to have regular health checks in middle age. Some, such as blood pressure tests, may be practised routinely by your doctor as you get older. Others, such as bone density scans, are specialized tests that may be performed if you are thought to be at particular risk of disease.

self checks

As you approach the menopause, keeping a diary of your periods and any physical and emotional symptoms you experience enables you to look for patterns and develop coping strategies. This information is also useful to your doctor. You should also perform a breast self-examination once a month and weigh yourself on a weekly basis to check that you are not gaining weight. If you are, you can take steps to lose it quickly.

blood cholesterol tests

Testing the blood for cholesterol is one way to assess your vulnerability to cardiovascular disease. If your blood cholesterol is too high, you can try to reduce it by making dietary changes. Blood cholesterol checks can be carried out by your doctor or it is possible to buy home-test kits.

blood pressure checks

Checking your blood pressure is a routine test that most doctors will carry out at regular intervals as you grow older. If your blood pressure is too high, you can try to reduce it through dietary changes, or your doctor may prescribe medication.

bone density scans

Postmenopausal women become more vulnerable to osteoporosis as they get older. Although it is not a routine health check, the best way to gain a picture of bone health is a specialized type of x-ray, known as a bone density scan. If you have already been diagnosed with osteoporosis, doctors may recommend bone density scans to assess the efficacy of any treatment you are having.

△ **By keeping a diary of health changes you may be able to give your doctor valuable information should their help be required.**

cervical smear tests

Cancer of the cervix affects younger women more than older women but, nevertheless, the cervical smear test remains an important diagnostic tool. It can show up precancerous changes in the cervix in women of all ages and action can be taken to prevent the cancer developing. You should have a cervical smear test every two or three years; more frequently if you have a history of genital warts.

If any abnormalities are detected during a cervical smear test, a doctor may perform a colposcopy. This is a technique that permits close-up inspection of the cervix at a microscopic level.

electrocardiograms

An electrocardiogram (ECG) is a specialized test that may be performed if your doctor suspects heart problems.

Electrodes applied to your body transmit electrical signals to a monitor. The signals appear as a trace on the monitor screen and provide detailed information about the contractions of the heart muscle.

eye tests

Because you become more susceptible to eye problems as you get older, it is important for you to visit an ophthalmologist annually. Eyesight problems can have serious repercussions with age and, when combined with weak bones, can increase the chances of falls and fractures.

hormone level tests

Testing the blood for the presence of elevated hormone levels can provide valuable information about the stage you are at in the menopause. For example, when the aging ovary fails to respond to follicle-stimulating hormone (FSH) the brain responds by releasing higher-than-usual amounts of FSH into the bloodstream. Hormone level tests are most likely to be performed by a gynaecologist.

mammography

The cure rate for breast cancer depends on the stage at which it is detected and whether or not it has spread. Mammography makes the early detection of breast cancer possible by providing an x-ray-type image that shows up changes in breast tissue. Mammograms are recommended every two years from the age of 45 (earlier if you have a family history of breast cancer).

other tests

There are other tests that your doctor may perform based on your individual medical history and current health. Both adult-onset diabetes and ovarian cancer, for example, can be detected by a blood test. You should try to keep abreast of the health tests that are available and ask your doctor about them.

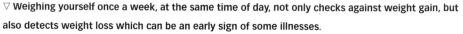
▽ Weighing yourself once a week, at the same time of day, not only checks against weight gain, but also detects weight loss which can be an early sign of some illnesses.

△ By performing breast examinations once a month, at the same point of the menstrual cycle, you will be able to detect any changes in the tissue at an early stage.

breast self-examination

It is important that you examine your breasts regularly, once a month at the end of your cycle if you are still menstruating, and at any time if you have ceased menstruation. Standing in front of a mirror, look for any changes in shape or texture of the breast tissue or around the nipples. Do this first with your arms by your sides and then with your hands raised behind you head.

Lie on your back with your shoulders slightly raised. With the fingers of your right hand gently examine your left breast in widening circles from the nipple outwards. Then, using your left hand, repeat the examination on your right breast. Finally, raise each arm behind your head in turn and check the armpits.

Consult your doctor if you notice any unusual lumps, dimples, nipple discharge, or the inversion of a previously normal nipple.

Complementary health

Practitioners of complementary health use a variety of diagnostic tools and techniques to assess health and detect illness. Some are the same as those used by conventional medical practitioners, others may be less familiar. For example, naturopaths use x-rays and blood tests in the diagnostic process. Practitioners of Chinese medicine are more likely to look at the colour of your skin, the colour and coating of your tongue and feel the rhythm and strength of the pulses at the wrists.

Index

acupuncture 11,52,61,68
alcohol 10,27,29,47,69
antioxidants 13,19,20,24,48
aromatherapy 61,63,69,74-75,81,92
arthritis 31,34,39,48-49,67,76

back problems 37,49,69
blood pressure 20,25,31,50,94
blood sugar 25,34,37
bones 46-49,94
breasts 87,92,94,95
breathing techniques 43,61
broken veins 72

caffeine 22,27,30,46-47,60
calcium 23,46-47,93
calories 16,25,26,28,29
cancer 13,16,20,21,24,26,52,91,94
carbohydrate 18,21,24-25,28,62
cardiovascular system 18, 19, 21, 27, 36,
    50-51,59,60,90
cholesterol 20,21,24,50,51,94
concentration, poor 88,92

dairy products 22-23,24,28,46
dehydration 26-27,73
depression 62-63,87,90,92
diabetes 18,31,50,55,79,94
diet 13,15-31,46,50,62,93
digestive system 47,52-53,63
drinks 26-27, 28,53,61

eating patterns 17,18,28,69
essential fatty acids 19,62,79
exercise 27,33-43,46,52,61,85
        aerobic 17,29,36-37,50,51
        anaerobic 36,38-39
        weight-bearing 36,47,90
eyesight 54-55,94

fats 18,19,20, 24,28,48,57
fibre 21,25,26,52
fish oils 16,19,20,24,48,50
flower remedies 61,68,87,92
fluid retention 20,25,89
food intolerance 21,22-23,31,48
foods, anti-aging 20-21

foot care 78-79
forgetfulness 88,92
free radicals 12-13,20,48,73
fruit 13,16,18,20,21,25,28,52,73

garlic 21,24,53
ginger 21,53

hair 34,80-81
hands 72,76-77
health checks 94-95
hearing problems 56-57
heart disease (see cardiovascular system)
herbalism 10-11,52-53,87,92
homeopathy 52,61,92
hormones 21,84-87,89,94 (see also HRT)
hot flushes 21,86,87,90,92
HRT 47,50,59,72,90-91

immune system 16,21,36,64
insomnia 67,68,88,90,92
massage 52,59,61,75,76,79,92
meat 18-19,24
menopause 31,58-59,72,81,83-93
menstrual cycle 84-85,94
minerals 21,27,73
        supplements 30-31,47,60
moisturizer 72,73,74,77,79
mood swings 58,87

naturopathy 51,52,95
night sweats 58,66-67,86,87,88,92
nuts 21,24,47,57

osteoporosis 21,25,31,36,46-47,90

Pilates method 42-43
pollution 10,12,30,73
positive thinking 8,61,64-65,85
protein 16,25,28,46

reflexology 11,51,56,61
relationships 9,58-59,65
relaxation 50,60-1,68-69,85,86,87

St John's wort 10,11,63,87
sex 58-59,88-89
skin 20,21,26,27,34,66,72-74,75
sleep 12,62,66-69,73,81
smell, loss of 57
smoking 12,30,47,51,68,72,73
snoring 68
stress 27,34,50,56,59,60-61
sugar 17,20,24-25,30,60
sun 10,12,72,73,76
supplements 13,30-31,47,48,60,93

taste, loss of 57
teeth 53
urinary problems 89

vaginal dryness 58,89,91
varicose veins 51
vegetables 13,16,18,20,47,52,73
vitamins 13,19,20,21,25,26,27,51,60,62,
63,73,74,79,89,93

water 25,26,27,28,29,72,73
weight loss 16-17,28-29,48,50,94

yoga 38,40-41,49,60-61,68,93

zinc 13,19,21,47,57,60,93